Home Cash Power. Thinking About Making Money Online?
Before you Do, You Need This Guide:
Step By Step Guide to Having Online Success Working From Home

By
Amaka C Adindu

Author page

Business Coach, Social Media Marketing Engagement Consultant. She have hands on experience from several years in business operations and management. Being an independent Business owner has its challenges she did experience all these challenging. There are so many issues to deal with on a day to day basis. She has called it a quit, because she chose a different part in life. She is passionate about working from home to be able to be with her 3 kids and have a chance to work in Network Marketing. She is open to all the thrills and satisfactions that comes with it, and believe her, there are plenty to go around. Having been an independent business owner she has learn so much in her adult life to last me a lifetime. Using what she have learn and the challenges involved in running an independent business. there is no better place for her to be at this moment but here at Home with her kids and managing a home based business. Starting a home based business is the real deal and it has its challenges. If you apply yourself you will learn how to work smarter instead of harder.

Using the right tools and connecting with the right people will make a huge change for anyone looking to change His or her life. Social media have come a long way and it is providing great resource to grow any business. She has Enthusiasm and she lives with Passion.

Making her DREAMS a REALITY!!

You have the power and the opportunity to change your life. You can make anything you want of it.

It's not difficult; it just takes some effort and determination. See things as you would have them be instead of as they are. Develop a personal plan that focuses on What you want, not on what you have. Your imagination will show you how to turn possibility into reality. Visualize your goals and your, Subconscious will work toward making that mental picture come true. When you picture yourself as winning that alone will contribute to your success. Knowing your destination is all you need to get there. Get a road map to your future in the form of vision board, life circle plan. Draw a plan of where you want to go and how you are going to get there. Make the steps... Thank you!

God Bless!

Social Media Site Connections:
Twitter: http://www.twitter.com/dreamtripscda
Facebook: https://www.facebook.com/empowermentoflives
Linkedin: http://www.linkedin.com/in/dreamtrips
Ibotoolbox: http://www.ibosocial.com/Dreamtrips
Google +: https://plus.google.com/+ChristineAdindu
Web site: http://www.onewaytobetterlife.com
Instagram: https://instagram.com/dreamtripscda/

Pinterest: http://www.pinterest.com/dreamtripscda/

SoundCloud: https://soundcloud.com/dreamteamonemarketing

Web site: http://www.onewaytobetterlife.com

Blog: http://www.socialknack.blog

Table of Contents

Introduction

Home Cash Power - Thinking about making Money Online working from home? Before you do, you need This Guide: Step By Step Guide to running a Home based business Online and or off line . These helpful tips will lead you on your way. It is possible to have a successful work from home business. Success depends on the inner drive to succeed coupled with the knowledge of how to achieve your goals. By using the advice provided in this book, you will see your income from your work from home business flourish.

Getting started on running home businesses is a terrific way to make income at home. But, this is not easy. You must understand how to run a successful business. This book provides you with that kind of help. Reading this book will inspire you to take your life into your own hands. You get a lot of tips about starting a home based business online and or off line. When you think about it now is the time to grab the bull by the horns and go for it! You can keep this book for reference to read anytime you are not sure what the next step you should be taking is. Follow all the tips put together and you will see success your home based business adventure.

Each chapter addresses different areas that you will run into in your home based business adventure. This allows you to tackle issues as they come up with solutions to deal with matters as they come up in your adventure. There are no yes or no answer to running a home business. But know what to do and how to handle matters related to your business as the arises will bring great success.

Chapter 1

Tremendous Opportunities Are Waiting For You With A New Home Business Enterprise

A lot of people dismiss this type of work as wishful thinking. If you know the tricks on how to work from your home, it's easier to run this type of business than you realize. This book is the go-to source for getting a home business enterprise up and running.

Join a few online forums and discussion groups that focus on the subject of online business. Search the internet and you will find a lot of great forums that you can become a part of. Blogs are a wonderful source of information.

You should get a post office box for all your business mailings. You don't want to use your home address when setting things up online. It can keep your identity and your family's identity protected.

People that run their own businesses at home enjoy a strong peer support group. Seek out other people and establish a network of support. It is not necessary to network with people selling the exact same item. But surrounding yourself with other motivated work from home business owners is helpful

When you are working from home, it is still important for you to be the best you can. Working from home can be fulfilling, but it can also be depressing if you don't approach it well. Continue to shower every morning, get regular exercise, and limit snacking. The tips below can help you feel more confident and others will see that!

Create an account at one of the many online business forums available on the internet. This allows you to find others who are in similar situations. Many home business enterprise owners have the same problems and it is good to have people to share concerns with.

Select a name for your business that holds personal value. Select an appropriate domain related to this business name as soon as you think of it. You can find a domain name for $10 a year but make sure you buy your domain name before anyone knows about your business. You should create a simple page with your contact information and put it online while you develop your website.

Make sure your home business meets local zoning laws and regulations. You may face shutdowns or fines if you don't. Even if you follow all the regulations, you have to be sure that you keep a low profile. Install any signs that are necessary, but don't go overboard. Invisibility is your goal.

Try using affiliates to promote your product or service. Swap affiliate links with like-minded business owners. Join other affiliate programs to see if they have products that are like yours. This will give you a great boost in profit without spending a lot of money.

As this book stated in the beginning, running a home based business is a dream for many people. Though many share this dream, few have a good idea about how to get started. This book is setup to provide you with all the advice and information you need to make a success of your own home business.

It is a smart strategy to start a home business.

Stop commuting, start a home based business today!

But, to many people, the concept appears too optimistic to put into practice. If you know the right approach to working from home, you may already be in a good position to start a home based business. This book contains many tips on work from home business that will give you much of the information you need to get started.

It is important that you dress for success, regardless of the physical location of where you work. It is easy when you work from home to just stay in your pyjamas all day. Getting dressed for work, just like in a normal business, can benefit you in the long run. Doing this will give you the right attitude to be as fruitful and creative as possible.

When choosing merchandise for your business it is wise to select those that you use yourself. For a product to sell it must fill a need consumers have that is not currently met. If you need certain products, there's a strong likelihood that others could use it as well.

Make your own website banner page. If you are on good terms with other businesses in your niche, see if you can set up a reciprocal linking arrangement. This provides more back links for boosting your search engine rankings. Helps potential customers find your site.

Reward customers who refer friends to your work from home business. People spreading the word about your business is an effective way to promote your business. When you show your customers that you are grateful for their help thanks to incentives, they will be more willing to help you.

Make use of affiliate marketing. Trade affiliate links with others. This is beneficial for both businesses. You can also join affiliate marketing programs and look to promote complementary products to your own. You can boost your revenues without the need to increase your inventory.

Communicate with your home based business customer base; share information without overwhelming them.

Let customers opt into updates through newsletters or an e-mail list. Send them updates on your business, or let them know about ongoing discounts and specials. While it's great to give out information, you should always take care not to send out too much.

Always set aside some of your profits for tax purposes. Business taxes range between 15%-20%, so put away about that much to avoid having to come up with it at the end of the year.

Take the time to talk to a business attorney around your area before you start your online business. There are sometimes specific laws about home businesses. Getting an expert legal opinion will ensure that you follow your local laws. To avoid any potential difficulties with your state government.

As noted back in the introduction, a home business enterprise is a dream that lots of people share. Unfortunately, the people who have this dream are people who will never learn. How to create their own successful home business. Use the helpful advice mentioned in this book, and you'll be running a successful work from home business in no time.

Chapter 2

Make Sure Your Home Business Enterprise Works For You

Simple Ideas That Lead To Better Performance

Whether you have just begun a home based business, or have had it for many years. There are new ideas always available about the best way to make it more efficient. The advice included here should help you see things in a new light.

You can get a tax deduction for your work from home business Internet costs. You can write off the Internet costs, but if you use it as a home connection as well, you cannot claim more than 50% the cost on you taxes. Read the rules on the IRS website.

If you need to "wine and dine" your clients, make sure that you deduct the cost of these meetings during tax time. These are legitimate business expenses and should to consider as such. Any expenses involving clients or potential clients are tax-deductible. Only when they can deemed as a paying or likely to pay in the future client, so exercise caution.

Do your absolute best to keep up with your personal needs when working at home. The flexibility of running a home based business can be a blessing. But, you still need to take time for yourself. You should take your showers in the morning, limit the amount of snacks you consume, and always make the time to get exercise. These tips can boost your view of yourself as well as how others see you!

Your business name should be strong and mean something to you. Select an appropriate domain related to this business name as soon as you think of it. A lot of domains run under $10; you want to secure yours before your competition does. Once you own your domain, create a single page with your contact information and a quick blurb on what you do or sell.

Obey all your local laws. You might end up with fines and embarrassing situations if you don't do this. Keep a low profile. That means little traffic and discreet signage. Stay invisible.

Gaining your family and friends' support is important when starting your home-based business. Operating a work from home business takes up a great deal of time, and can be fraught with hardships and stress. If your family members are not willing to help and support you, even just by giving you alone time to work. You will not be able to run a home business enterprise.

Choose a name with meaning. Because your brand name serves as an ambassador to your products. You should make sure that your name is recognizable to assist your customers in relating to you. The name you pick may have an interesting or unique story associated with it. This can help you and your brand become something that customers can come to appreciate and support for years to come.

Thinking is critical to business, so finding answers to the questions you may not have known you had can spur a great journey. Preparing for unexpected circumstances ensures you will never face any hardship you cannot handle. Continue to learn, and you will have a evolving home based business online and or off line.

Always apply Home Business Enterprise Basics, Easy Ideas For Successful Entrepreneurs

Just like everything else running a business from home can be hard work, but it has a lot of advantages, too. This type of business pays off according to the time you put into it at first. In time, your business will come into its own, but in the beginning, you may feel like you are failing. Perseverance and the information you find below is necessary to make it work.

One type of deduction you might be able to get is for an internet connection. You can claim a part of the total cost of these services for business purposes.

It's healthy to take short breaks over the course of your work day. Don't use your break time to take care of complicated personal matters, but. For instance, don't do house chores or make personal calls. Rejuvenate and empower yourself with short activities that wake you up. Like a brief stint with exercise or quick weeding of your garden.

You must be ready and conscientious to run successful home businesses. Since many regulations apply to buildings and businesses. Check with your county to make sure the set-up you have in mind for your work from home business does not create any legal conflict. You may find a separate office building on your property to be most suitable. Setting aside a dedicated space for your home office will keep you focused on your work.

Make sure you let people know if you are out of a certain product. It's upsetting to order an item and find that you won't receive it for weeks. Give your clients the option to chose other products and let them know when a product is on back-order.

You need a post office box for business mail. Don't ever publish your home address online. Taking this step allows you and your family to remain anonymous.

An office is necessary when you based at home for work purposes. Your office doesn't need to be huge, but it does need to be inviting. It should be somewhere you will be productive and efficient. Don't concern yourself with the total size; you can work with any size space.

Through online message boards, you can find support from different home business owners. For improving your work from

home business. There is a huge number and variety of sites and forums for home business owners. The support and understanding is invaluable. You could find mentors on these forums that can provide you with their wisdom and understanding.

Define your niche in details. Finding the right audience for your goods and services is essential. Once done, making sales will become easier. Ask all those you know, whether friends, business peers, or customers, what they think of your niche. See if they can give you referrals. Attend trade shows for your industry and see who is buying, then follow up with them.

Even though it may seem like it's not worth it, many businesses started the same way. Overnight success does not come to anyone in this field. Hard work helps your business foundation become strong. Stay focused, determination is your key and have a goal to what it is you want to achieve and work towards that goal.

Chapter 3

Guide To Success For Your Work From Home Business

Many people seem to think that this is difficult to do. If you know how to go about it, operating a successful home based business of your own may be quite possible. Read this book to find out how you can get started.

For example, if you entertain clients by eating out with them, you can deduct this from your taxes. These are legitimate business expenses and one should treated as such. Be careful, but make sure that such meetings are with paying or potential clients. , because otherwise meals and entertainment are not tax-deductible expenses.

To make your home-business venture profitable, you need ingenuity and ambition. You may want to consider renting or building an office for your business. This would be helpful if you will have face to face contact with customers. This also helps you make a clean break between your home and business life.

If you have trouble thinking of the right product to sell, imagine something that you find useful in your everyday life. Finding a specific need that is not yet met, is key to a successful business. The higher the chance that you could use an item or service, the higher the chance others could use that item or service too.

If one of your products is not available for any reason, post that information on your website. It's upsetting to order an item and then find out that the shipment will take weeks or longer. Avoid selling products that are out of stock; if they are, inform your customers so that they are not left waiting while you restock.

One option of earning money from home is to offer lessons in a skill that you have. A lot of people prefer to take lessons instead of through a school with rigid schedules. You can teach hobby-related lessons, for things like photography or music, out of your home.

When you working from home, limit your family interruptions. Set strict working hours and make sure that family and friends know exactly when they are in force. It is important that they understand that privacy needed and will allow you to spend time with them just as soon as you complete your work. Make sure children supervised and that you can contacted in an emergency.

You will find a lot of good advice about home business enterprise ownership on the Internet. But, be aware of the many home business enterprise scams advertised on the Internet. Some websites sell information that you can gained elsewhere for free. Offer pricey courses on basic techniques. Some scams lure their victims into paying for access to high-quality work that does not exist. While others may provide fake online classes. If it is sound too good, it is not true.

So many people these days have a dream of being their own boss. Though many share this dream, few have a good idea about how to get started. Take it one step at a time, apply the tips from this book. Soon you will find yourself the proud owner of a brand-new home business enterprise. Be open to learning as the saying goes knowledge is power you income grows with it. With that said keep in mind knowledge is power if applied to achieve your goal.

One of the key thing for most business owners are how to apply what they have learned and make the best of it. I find that books like this one gives you the basis of what you need to do at first. But over time you want to put your self in the position to learn more and grow. Your end goal is to get the largest profits for you with low investment and adding extra time to you home business project.

Explore the tricks for Home Businesses.

There is a wealth of information available to help get you started with your own home business enterprise. Don't just buy everything that's out there. This book is a must as far as reliable information goes, so read on.

Be sure and order a separate line for your home business enterprise communications.

This helps avoid you answering the good phone manner helps customers see it as a business.

Make your home office as comfortable as possible, and stock it with all necessary supplies. This may seem silly or trivial, but you'll need a comfortable office and the right supplies to be able to get to work.

Look for price ranges for a product in today's market before you start trying to sell. Set your prices based off competitor evaluations so you can be competitive in your offering. When you are attempting to make a sale, avoid putting down the competition. Emphasize the benefits of your product or service instead.

A good way to gather information on running a home business is join an online forum on the topic. Joining a forum will give you a chance to exchange pertinent information with your business peers. Many people who work from home will have the same issues and problems as you, so you can share solutions.

Get together a list of the things you wish to do everyday. Some things you may not be able to get to, but do set goals everyday so that you can do it whenever possible. Set limits and boundaries when working from home to generate respect.

Make sure that you are not breaking any laws or ordinances in your area. If you don't, you may end up paying out of business or charged hefty fines, and that can be quite embarrassing. Also remember that a neighbor-friendly attitude goes right along with it. Making sure you follow with the letter of the law. In part, that means discreet signage and least noise and traffic. Do not call undue attention to your house.

An online business is a real business, so don't go charging in without a business plan. You can change this or disregard it at any time. Use this type of a plan as a to-do list of sorts and as a beacon for guiding you to your end goal. It is important to update your business plan from time to time.

The best financial strategy for a work from home business is to take advantage of as many tax deductions that you can justify. Look for and claim every deduction that you can, and enjoy a lower tax bill.

Consult with a lawyer that deals in business before you launch your work from home business. Certain states have particular laws when it comes to starting a home business enterprise. A business lawyer can help see if you are following those laws so that you don't get in trouble.

Some of this information is not news to you. Gurus have been selling their business "secrets" for a long time. Home business enterprise uses the same principles that all businesses do. But you must be well-informed to succeed. Stay informed. Leave no stone unturned, learn as much as you can. The knowledge you gain will take you a long way into your home business adventure.

Chapter 4

In this chapter we are going address how you can get your Home Based Business Going. By applying these helpful tips

Think about what your life would be like if you worked for the man or woman instead of yourself. It may be your sole income source or perhaps a terrific supplement. This book will give you ideas about how to grow your business into a prosperous enterprise.

If you need to have the Internet to run your business, know that you can get tax deductions. You can deduct a part of the price of any service that provides that sort of function. Although the cap of that part is 50 percent if you also use it for purposes other than business.

If you must take clients out, you can itemize these expenses. The IRS and/or Revenue Agency counts these types of meetings as business expenses that are deductible. Be careful not to deduct your normal dining expenses. Though; only eating out with potential or actual clients are deductible.

If a product that you sell is no longer in stock, say so on your website. Let your customers know the status of their order. If you are out of stock, let them know. When a product is on back-order, make it clear so that customers have the opportunity to choose a suitable substitute.

Try to limit family interruptions while you are on the clock. When you are interrupted while working, you will be less productive. Make everyone aware when you are working and when you will be done. Explain that you need privacy so that you can be available to them sooner. Be certain that your children are in good care, and that you can be contacted if there is an emergency.

When you start a home based business, seek out people who will support you. You can start your own alliance or find one that exists near by. Even though these people might not be in your niche, you all are alike in your motivations to succeed.

Your website needs a banner page. This will give you the ability to trade links with other companies. This provides more back links for boosting your search engine rankings. Helps potential customers find your site.

Starting a checking account for your business will help keep track of your records more. Make sure all orders and expenses go through this account. This way, you have a detailed record of all money that flows through your business. It is also a good idea to open a specific credit card for your business.

When it comes tax time, you want to make sure that you are taking all the deductions and credits available. That you can qualify for. If you claim all the tax deductions you can, your tax bill will be a lot lower.

Big money in online business comes from experimenting and taking risks. When you are willing to try new things in your business, you will find more people interested in what you are doing. Which means a bigger bottom line! Unless you try new things in your routine, you may miss out on better, more effective options.

Always make sure your online business keeps running to make more profits and to feel accomplished. We hope that the advice you have found here will help you maximize your business now and in the future. Getting help with your home based business is essential and it is prelude to success.

When it comes to starting and running home businesses, it is a terrific way to make income from home. But, this isn't easy. You must understand how to run a successful business. This book provides you with that kind of help.

Have a pithy sound bite to describe your business. If you can explain what you business does in a few words, you will likely impress clients in a meeting and attract customers. This will help you come up with a slogan that expresses your business' main aim.

Your focus should be to please all your customers. It is easier to get sales from satisfied repeat customers than people who have never purchased anything from you. When you please your customers, they will come back.

Create a schedule that dedicates specific hours to your home business enterprise. Other hours to your personal life. It is important to have a set stopping point each day. Be sure to schedule personal time, as well as time to socialize with your friends and family.

Your website should updated when your stock of a particular product runs out. Customers are certain to upset with you if the products they ordered will take weeks to arrive to them. When a product is on back-order, make it clear so that customers have the opportunity to choose a suitable substitute.

You should make it a priority to get a post office box for routing your business mail to, as opposed to your current address. Do not give out your family's home address online, even for your business. This will help protect the identities of you and your family.

Save money by keeping good records about any expenditures you make for your business. Internet service and car mileage related to your business are a couple examples of business expenses. Being an owner and operator of your own business, your expenses have expenses of their own that can take off your taxes. There is no reason to give your money away to the government. Keep track of all those little expenses. They could add up to big savings.

Always look toward the future. It is important to celebrate past successes, but they have already happened. Your focus needs to be what is waiting in the coming days and weeks. Keeping your mind on the future will make it easier for you to know what you need to capitalize on, and what obstacles may be coming. You are sure to to be ready when any comes your way.

Promoting your home based business online can be simple once you've got the skills and concepts down. One great option may be to set up a website to promote your online business. You can set up the website on your own within a day. You can register your domain for free in some cases, but most cost a small fee to register them. Your profits can make it well worth the little expense.

As mentioned before, running a work from home business may generate real income if you know the tricks. If you keep the information shared here in mind and apply the advice to your own business, the sky is the limit.

Chapter 5

If you have the option to go your Own Way with these work from home tips and ideas. Here are some Work From Home Business Secrets to apply.

It is exciting when you start your own home based business. Many people wish they could be in charge of their own business. When you are, but, you need to remember you are a professional to maximize your business potential. This book has plenty of information about running a successful home business enterprise.

If an Internet connection is in used to run your business, you can deduct it on your taxes. While internet service is tax deductible. It is important to remember that only a part of the expense is deductible if used for purposes other than business.

Keep your focus on maintaining your relationship with current customers. You need a lot less effort to get repeat sales than new sales. A happy customer base will return again and again.

Make sure you create a mailing list as your home based business grows. Maintain healthy communications, but avoid becoming "spammy" and losing the customer. Use your mailing list to distribute news of promotions you are running. Some people also use mailing lists to send coupons. Relevant information and articles to their customers as often as possible. Your website should have a sign up section for new users that come to your site and interested in joining the mailing list.

Make a business plan for your work from home business. No matter the size of your business, make sure you plan out your goals and how you will get there. A business plan helps you stay on track as you grow your business.

Affiliate marketing can provide great benefits. Let other home businesses know about your affiliate links and they may share theirs. Join affiliate programs and find out if you can be an affiliate for products which complement yours. This is a great way to increase the range of products you offer without having to add more inventory.

A home based business is a business like any other, so it is crucial that you keep good financial records of everything. If you end up audited by tax authorities like the IRS, you are going to have to show records and proof of your expenses and income. Good records also allow you to keep track of your business and how well it is doing from month to month.

When you first establish your online business, you need to estimate initial costs. Home businesses do not cost as much as traditional businesses, but there will still be costs you will need to take into account. Find out how much money it costs to keep your business running is important. As it will allow you to see how much you will be spending in the long term.

You are the only one responsible for success or failure when you create a online business for yourself. It doesn't have to be an onerous responsibility though. If you do your homework to learn what you need to know, and further, put in the work to success, there are many advantages. Using the powerful advice above can be just what you need to grow and succeed.

What You Need To Know About A Work From Home Business

It seems like everyone is wanting to run a business from home, but most people aren't sure what they need to do to get started. You don't have to be unfamiliar about home businesses anymore. If so, read on to learn some of the do's and don'ts when it comes to running a online business.

If you have to drive a lot for your business, make sure you track your gas mileage and keep receipts for whatever gas you use. Any business related travel expenses you incurred you can claim at tax time.

You need to be sure that you're able to prove that the trips had to do with your business.

Find the best way to describe your business through a sound bite. Keeping things simple and to the point will help to catch people attention. This statement also provides you with a ready-made base for a slogan. As it will already cover the important points of your business.

You need a backup plan just in case your online business doesn't go well. Have plans for things like issues with your web host and missing product shipments. When you prepared for things going wrong you won't caught short if you lose your income.

Do appropriate background checks on potential employees. Likewise, verify their employment references. Poor employees can turn a successful fledgling business into a flop. So be sure that you hire reliable people with the skills needed to help your company grow.

You need a post office box for business mail. Do not give out your family's home address online, even for your business. This helps safeguard your identity as well as the identity of your family.

Cut family interruptions during your home work hours. Too many interruptions can make hinder your ability to work. so always let loved ones know when you will be working as well as when you will finish. They should understand that your privacy and work focus is key to making money so they can eat and have a roof over their heads. Be sure that your kids have supervision and your sitter is able to reach you in case something goes wrong.

Include a banner bar for your site. You will be able to exchange for your banners with outer web masters. Having credible links on your site will improve your search engine rankings.

One of the most important considerations when you are running a business from your home. Is to make the most of deductions you are claiming are for the business. Claiming every deduction for which you qualify on your taxes can save you a sizable amount of money.

It is important to have a detailed business plan before you put a lot of time and money into a business. Write a plan and seek professional input. They will give you an goal analysis. A solid plan will allow you to get down to business and effectively. After your entity launched, the details you can iron out.

You now have a more in-depth understanding of owning your own home-based business. Using these tips is the best way to get started. So do just that, and success should come before you know it.

Here are extra Tips And Tricks For A Successful Home Business

Enterprise that you can apply today.

Keep your goal in mind.

You should know that there are so many great opportunities when it comes to home based business, online business. The benefits of time flexibility and control over your destiny is a major draw. Most people never make it from the dreaming stage to the execution. Follow these tips if you are serious about starting and running your own successful home based business.

Because any home based business can fail, you must start yours while you are still employed. It takes a while to start making any money, so if you can keep your income from work, that will help. Being able to pay the bills and keep cash in your bank account will make you more comfortable while waiting for your business to take off.

To better track your business-related spending, open a specific checking account for your business. Use the account for all your company's financial transactions, including sales profits and expenses. This makes it easier to track your company's transactions. Also, you should only use a credit card that is designated for the business to order supplies or conduct other business transactions.

Make sure your work from home business meets local zoning laws and regulations. Fines may result if you do not abide by the regulations in place. Maintain a good standing in your neigbour hood both by following the laws and keeping a low profile. In part, that means discreet signage and least noise and traffic. Don't draw too much attention.

Your home business needs a business plan, even if it's just something you're doing on the side.

Even small home businesses need to have delineated goals. A good picture of any needed resources and some strategies for meeting the goals. Having a plan in place will help you stay on top as your business grows.

Make sure that you're getting all the tax benefits that you can when you are running a business. There are large savings to be had with claiming as many deductions as you can on your taxes.

Deposit your payments when you receive them. Consider making daily bank deposits rather than monthly or weekly. If you don't deposit a check right away, it could get lost. Always use a teller to make deposits instead of the ATM, because this ensures that all questions taken care of answered.

Although it may be difficult to resist giving customers special breaks or leniency. When you are first building up your business. This can be a dangerous practice for your bottom line. Make sure you set up payment terms that are clear for all your invoices and documents. Along with a reasonable penalty, like eight percent, over what the invoice amount is. If the total isn't paid within the normal payment terms.

As you can see, it will need a little bit of work and dedication to make the jump. If you can manage to pull through and stick to the plan. You will be able to represent your dream in the company's image. And create something that is long-lasting and profitable over the years. Don't hesitate to get help with your home Based Business. The idea of starting and running home businesses is a terrific way to make extra income. A way to gain at home and gain the tax benefit associated with running a home based business. It is clear that the idea is not easy for anyone. You must understand a few basic steps on how to run a successful business.

As mentioned this book provides you with that kinds of help you could imagine at the beginning.

What business are you in? have a pithy sound bite to describe your business. If you can explain what you business does in a few words, you will likely impress clients in a meeting and attract customers. This will help you come up with a slogan that expresses your business' main goal.

Your focus should be to meet all your customers and your clients. It is easier to get sales from satisfied repeat customers than people who have never purchased anything from you. When you please your customers, they will come back and they will talk about your product and refer others to your business. Customer's satisfaction is your top priority.

Make a schedule that dedicates specific hours to your home business enterprise. Other hours to your personal life. It is important to have a set stopping point each day. Be sure to schedule personal time, as well as time to socialize with your friends and family. "All work and no play...." you need to know how to balance your time with other things in your personal life.

If you have a website you should updated when your stock of a particular product runs out. That is if you are selling products, and if your are offering services make prompt service is available to your clients. Customers are certain to be unhappy with you if the products they ordered will take weeks to arrive to them and or service.

They requested is not on time as per scheduled. When a product is on back-order, make it clear so that customers have the opportunity to choose a suitable substitute. When service order is over the scheduled time make sure the customer know that as well. If for any reason there is a change in the scheduled time be sure to notify the customer. You have to put yourself in the position of the customer and reason with your customer.

You should make it a priority to get a post office box for routing your business mail to, as opposed to your current address. Do not give out your family's home address online, even for your business.

This will help protect the identities of you and your family.

This is just a security measure for you and your family. You are dealing with the public.

You can save money by keeping good records about any expenditures you make for your business. Internet service and car mileage related to your business are a couple examples of business expenses. Being an owner and operator of your own business, your expenses have expenses of their own that you can remove off your taxes. There is no reason to give your money away to the government. Keep track of all those little expenses.

They could add up to big savings for you. Consult with your professional accountant about tax-deductible expenses

Always look toward the future with a positive mind set. It is important to celebrate past successes, but they have already happened. Your focus needs to be what is waiting in the coming days and weeks.

Keeping your mind on the future will make it easier for you to know what you need to capitalize on. What obstacles may be coming, you cannot cut surprises that may come your way.

Promoting your home based business online and off line can be simple once you've got the skills and concepts down. One great option may be to set up a website to promote your business online and off line. You can set up the website on your own within a day. You can register your domain for free in some cases, but most cost a small fee to register them. Your profits can make it well worth the little expense.

As mentioned before, running a work from home business may generate real income if you know the tricks are to follow. If you keep the information shared here in mind and apply the advice to your own business. You should see progressive result and the sky is the limit to what you can achieve.

Chapter 6

Running A Home Based Business Is Easy When You've Got Great Tips!

A lot of people are under the impression that it is difficult to start a work from home business. They say the income you make is unstable and that it should considered more as a part time job than a full time one. This does not need to be the case! Take a look at these great tips that can help you get a profitable one started.

Update your website if your inventory has run out on individual products. Customers will respect your honesty, and will be more apt to do future business with you. When a product is on back-order, make it clear so that customers have the opportunity to choose a suitable substitute.

Join message boards and forums about your niche and home businesses in general. This will help you network in your industry and establish your product and name. Someone you meet there could help you build your profits!

A business aim is a short description of your business and what it does. This allows you to provide an explanation about your business and where you intend for it to go. You also need to explain what factors set your business apart from the competition. What goals you hope to achieve in your business venture.

All businesses should have an emergency fund. You will be able to pay for expenses you are not expecting. Do not dip into an emergency fund if it is not necessary to do so, and when you do have to take money out of it, try to replace it as soon as possible.

Check with a tax professional to find out which tax deductions allowed. To be sure what your home business enterprise can get refunds on and make sure to take them. Claiming every deduction for which you qualify on your taxes can save you a sizable amount of money.

Self-promoting is the key to gaining exposure and building your home business enterprise up. Promoting is a large part of success in home businesses. Stressing the high quality of your products is essential in attracting your customers. Understanding how to sell yourself and your company is a primary key to success.

Keep your mind focused on what is yet to come. Remember that those successes are the past. Tomorrow, next week, and further in the future is what needs your focus. This will help you to prepare for any future opportunities or possible obstacles along the way. By doing this, you won't find yourself surprised.

As you learn more, you will find that promoting your business isn't as hard as you once thought. Setting up a professional looking website is a good first step, and doesn't cost that much. It just takes a day to put up your own website. It is often possible to register domains for free, but most others are cheap. But, it can be worth the price if you make a profit.

Keeping the information here in mind and following through with it will show that running a business from home is possible. Determination is the key for the success of your business. Using the powerful tips here, you can earn a good living without ever leaving your home. It is exciting when you start your own home based business. As I mentioned earlier many people wish they could be in charge of their own business. When you are, but, you need to remember you are a professional to maximize your business potential. This book has plenty of information about running a successful home business enterprise.

Again if an Internet connection used to run your business, you can deduct it on your taxes. While internet service is tax deductible. It is important to remember that only a part of the expense is deductible if used for purposes other than business.

Consult with a tax professional about your benefit and a list of expenses that are tax deductible.

Keep your focus on maintaining your relationship with current customers and clients. You need a lot less effort to get repeat sales than new sales. A happy customer base will return again and will send referrals your way. If possible give incentives to your customers for referrals.

Make sure you create a mailing list as your home based business grows. Maintain healthy communications, but avoid becoming "spammy" and losing the customer. Use your mailing list to distribute news of promotions you are running. Example discounts on new items, give out samples, credit coupons. Some people also use mailing lists to send coupons. Relevant information and articles to their customers. Your website should have a sign up section for new users that want to joining the mailing list. Give them a reason to join your mailing list, a gift of some kind, something of value.

Make a business plan for your work from home business, making a plan needed. It servers as a guideline for you business and future projections. Review and change your plan as needed buy doing this you will see your business will shape up over time. No matter the size of your business, make sure you plan out your goals and how you will get there. A business plan helps you stay on track as you grow your business.

Affiliate marketing can provide great benefits. Let other home businesses know about your affiliate links and they may share theirs. Join affiliate programs and find out if you can be an affiliate for products which complement yours. This is a great way to increase the range of products you offer without having to add extra inventory.

A home based business is a business like any other, so it is crucial that you keep good financial records of everything. If you end up audited by tax authorities like the IRS, you are going to have to show records and proof of your expenses and income. Good records also allow you to keep track of your business and how well it is doing from month to month.

When you first establish your online business, you need to estimate initial costs. Home businesses do not cost as much as traditional businesses, but there will still be costs you will need to take into account. Find out how much money it costs to keep your business running this is important. As it will allow you to see how much you will be spending in the long term.

You are the only one responsible for success or failure when you create a online business for yourself. It doesn't have to be an onerous responsibility though. If you do your homework to learn what you need to know, and further, put in the work to success, there are many advantages. Using the powerful advice above can be just what you need to grow and succeed.

Chapter 7

Seeking Information About Running A Business At Home? Look Here!

A majority of people feel that the idea is unobtainable for them. If you know the tricks on how to work from your home, it's easier to run this type of business than you realize. This book contains many tips on online business that will give you much of the information you need to get started.

Have a "sound bite" description of your business ready in your mind. To keep the attention of customers, keep your description clear and concise. This also helps generate a slogan and make sure important points about your business covered.

Going above and beyond what expected will show your customers that you care. Always take the extra step. Include freebies with their order, or include a letter thanking them for their business. Adding these little touches can make your customer feel appreciated. They will feel that they are not used.

Keep your work and your personal life separate by establishing set working hours. Establish a cut-off time, and stop answering business calls after that time. To lead a balanced lifestyle, you need to set time aside for things besides work such as yourself and your family.

Be sure to keep your website up to date on which products are available and which, if any, are out of stock. Customers find it especially frustrating when orders they've placed will not fulfilled. For several days and not even for weeks. This is why you should allow your customers to have the opportunity to select another product. If their product is on back-order. Let them know before they place their order.

Your website should include a banner page. Such a page will give you the opportunity to swap banner links and similar advertisements with affiliated websites. This is a great way to increase your rankings and is simple.

If you are an artist, you may want to offer graphic design services to area businesses. Most small businesses prefer independent contractors because of their flexibility and lower prices. This will give you an advantage.

Your home business needs a business plan, even if it's just something you're doing on the side. Even with a small business, you need to document all your goals, strategies, and resources. Following a business plan helps you stay focused as your company grows.

Safety is important in your workplace. Smoke detectors and fire extinguishers are a must. You should also find an efficient solution to backup all your data. This can keep you safe and reduce injuries.

Before establishing your home business enterprise, you should speak with a local business attorney. Many states have laws about home businesses. Taking time to talk to a business lawyer will help you figure out what steps you have to take to operate your business by the books.

As the beginning of this book mentioned, many people dream about running their own home based business. Unfortunately, it is also true that so many people feel overwhelmed at the thought, with no idea of where to start. Use the advice found here to make that dream a reality. Be the proud owner of a profitable home based business whether online or offline.

In this paragraph we are going to explore some great Solutions for managing a Work From Home Business.

The tough economic times may be continuing for a long time. Joblessness is up and businesses are closing their doors nationwide. Things may seem bleak in this depression, but there are ways to make the most of it. Continue reading to learn how to come out on top, despite the recent economy.

A serious commitment to success is necessary for any home business enterprise. You may want to build your own home office that your customers can enter, since many counties have office regulations.

You can also keep your home life better divided from your work life if they happen in different buildings!

It's vital that distractions from friends and family eliminated when running a home business. Too many interruptions can hinder your ability to work. So always let loved ones know when you will be working as well as when you will finished. Tell them that you need to have privacy so you can finish work and then be available that much sooner. Make sure children will supervised and that they can reach you in an emergency.

You should let all your friends and relatives know about your business venture. To get your business off the ground, start with offering a discount or freebie. Encourage them to spread the word about your new business. There is nothing quite as effective as personal referrals.

Create a checking account for your business transactions. To be effective, you must ensure that you use the account for all your business expenses. You will get a better idea of your progress. Also, you should only use a credit card designated for the business. For purchased order supplies or conduct other business transactions.

Keeping careful track of each one of your business expenses is a vital way to protect your pocketbook. This involves everything from fuel used for business trips to your internet service. The great thing about these business-related expenses is that you can deduct some of them off your taxes. Even if you think the amount is too small, include it anyway, instead of giving it to the government, claim it.

For your business should have a short description. Explaining what your business is and what it does. You should state exactly what your goals are with your business and what it is about. This succinct statement should describe what makes your business model unique. Explain your plan and hope to achieve it.

Make sure that you have written a business plan for your home-based business. No matter the size of your business, make sure you plan out your goals and how you will get there. Following a business plan helps you stay focused as your company grows.

Make sure that you are comfortable flaunting yourself when you start a home business enterprise. You are going to have to be able to sell your product to a lot of people who may buy from you; that is one of the jobs of a business owner. Stressing the high quality of your products is essential in attracting your customers. Successful self-promotion is what leads to big profits in the business world.

As before stated, the current economy is not in good shape. This could be the answer to all your financial problems. Keep the information shared here in mind, and you will make and a create a successful business.

When it comes to making A Success Of Your Work From Home Business. Lots of folks have discovered the benefits of launching home businesses in a great way. But, there is always competition when it comes to having a home based business. It's imperative that you do your homework to learn how to be a success and keep your business running well. This way you will be able to lead the pack.

If you need to do any driving to meet the needs of your home based business. Keep detailed records of mileage and save all fill-up receipts. These fall into travel expenses, which you can get back come tax season. But, you must be able to prove that your driving was a necessary part of the business.

Starting a business that you can work on from home can be enjoyable and challenging at the same time. Find your niche, your area of expertise, and go from there. There are no limits to what you can decide, but you should know a good amount of information on the topic. Do your homework before making a commitment to any one project. It is also a wise idea to network with other people who have a successful home business.

Set a clear work schedule for yourself and use it to separate your home life from your business life. Determine an ending time for each workday. Take the time to enjoy yourself with your family and friends.

You must have a professional office set up in your home with all the equipment. Include supplies needed, when running a home-based business. It may seem silly, but if you are not comfortable and have all you need, you may not be productive.

Consider items that would interested you. If you are using in your own life if you are trying to decide what product to sell. Selecting a product that will be successful involves thinking about people's needs. If it improves your way of life, it stands to reason others can enjoy from it as well.

Having a separate account for your business finances makes record keeping much easier. Make all business-related transactions using this account. This enables you to analyze all your company's financial transactions. Also to the checking account, you'll need a credit card. For the business, such as purchases you can't make with a check.

You should always be looking forward. It is important to celebrate past successes, but they have already happened. You need to look to the future, and what is going to happen then. This can help you prepare for things that will happen in the future. That way, you won't be any surprised by something you weren't looking forward to seeing in the process.

Review your target market before starting your home business enterprise. Even if your knowledge about your product is on point.

When you know your target market you can better tailor your sales and marketing strategies so you attract buyers. When you design your website, keep in mind how customers usually buy your product or service.

There may be unwritten rules you do not know about.

With hard work, the tips shared here with you will allow your business to grow and succeed. It's important to keep up with the things that will make your business grow. Find all the information you can and use it to create a unique business strategy.

Chapter 8

One of the goals! Earn Some Extra Cash With A Home Business

There are circumstances beyond your control that can make life difficult. It's up to you to figure out how you will respond to those circumstances. You may wind up unemployed after working for years, leaving you in a quandary about what to do. Has the idea of a home-based enterprise ever occurred to you? By reading the book and the information in this chapter. You will be able to get some important information that you will need when becoming your own boss.

If your online home based business is your main source of income. Make sure you have some sort of back-up plan in the event that things don't go as planned. This is important to always have a secondary plan (PlanB) you can put into action in the case of a disaster. Planning for the worst means you will be able to handle it if it occurs.

Creating a home business enterprise is fun but challenging to do. You must first identify a niche for your business. Finding something that you already know about, or interested in, can help you to be successful. Before you rely on a single business, do your research. Use networking tools to learn from others who have been successful with creating a home business.

Keep track of all manufacturing costs, such as materials, labour and time. For products which you produce, as doing so you can prevent yourself from losing money. Basic wholesale prices would be twice that of cost. Commercial retailers then, double the price they paid the wholesaler. This ensures that everyone profits. Make it a fair price both you and the customers can agree upon.

When working from home, try to always achieve your personal best. Being successful in a home business is rewarding. But, make sure you still have your personal time despite not leaving the house. Working in your pyjamas is wonderful but don't make a habit of it. Get up, have a shower, and dress for the day as you would for any other work location. You can feel better about yourself and boost the way people look at you.

Select a name for your business that holds personal value. Even if you have not yet planned for a business website, buy your business domain name. You can find a domain name for $10 a year but make sure you buy your domain name before anyone knows about your business. Just put up one page for now until you decide if you want to expand to a full website.

While reading this book, you have in possession a lot of inspired ideas to take your life into your own hands. You have great tips here a lot of it about starting a online business. Now is the time to grab the bull by the horns and go for it! You can keep this book for reference to read anytime you are not sure what the next step you should be taking is.

Chapter 9

A Little Expert Guidance For Successful Home Based Business

You need to have a good foundation for an online business and or home based business, just as you do your house. The following information intended to provide you with a few basics of planning. Conceptualizing the foundation, and helping you to pull all the things you need. To get a good work from home business plan put into action.

If you need to do any driving to meet the needs of your home based business. Keep detailed records of mileage and save all fill-up receipts. Such expenses are deductible. You must be honest about it. The IRS Or Revenue agency could asked you provide a proof that your deductions are vital for your business.

Building a business at home is fun, although challenging. You must first identify a niche for your business. Try to find something that you are good at and have knowledge in already. Do a lot of research before deciding what kind of business you want to launch. Network with others who have home businesses to get some great ideas and tips.

When working from home, remember to keep on top of your personal appearance. Even though it can be fulfilling to have a home business enterprise. Your self-esteem could suffer if you place work before your own needs. Keep yourself clean, eat well, and work out daily. Apply this advice to improve your appearance and yourself image.

All home office workers need some type of office in their home. There's no need for an over sized office. But, the area must be professional, comfortable and used only for work. Your office

needs to be somewhere you feel productive, calm and inspired. Size should be less of a concern, as space can change at any time.

A good way to gather information on running a home business enterprise is to join an online forum on the topic. This allows you to find others who are in similar situations. Most people who work from home face the same difficulties and challenges. Discussing them is beneficial to all parties.

Create a fund for emergencies to help guard your business's financial well-being. Having an emergency fund will help cover surprise expenses. That will not causing your business operations to sputter. Only withdrawal money from the emergency fund when an emergency occurs. Remember you are only borrowing money from yourself.

Write a comprehensive business plan to guide the strategy of your online business. You can change this plan if you need to. This plan will help you get organized and go through the process of creating a business with a clear goal in mind. Keep your business plan updated often and changes arises.

Use these tips outlined above as part of your educational resources that will help you create and flesh out a business plan. Make it one that will support your efforts to set up and perpetuate a successful home based and online business. Your success in your work from home business will always need hard work. Using the tips above and in all the pages of this book can help you. Put your efforts towards actions that will likely produce positive results. Your home based business and online business needs hard work and dedication. Your online presence is crucial to your success.

It does not end there, there a do's and don'ts. When It Comes to starting and running a Home Based Business whether online or offline the same applies.

There is a plethora of information available to help you run your home business enterprise online or offline. Take time to decide what products to sale. Not every item is going to give you the success that you want. This book is a must as far as reliable information goes, so read on and always refer to this book for quick references as needed.

Take regular breaks throughout your day, but don't get distracted by the home environment. Don't take long, personal phone calls or start complicated home improvement projects. Refresh your mind and body with active breaks like a short session of exercise or working in the garden.

If one of your products is not available for any reason, post that information on your website. Back-ordered products are a nuisance to customers, and it can upset them. Mark out of stock items, so that they can choose something they'll receive sooner.

Limit the interruptions from your family when working from a home office. When you plan to work, let your family know you are not to interrupted, but also let them know when you'll be available again. They should understand that you need a private work environment so you can finish and spend time with them sooner. Be certain that your children are with supervised care. Let them know that they can contacted, and that they are able to reached you if there is an emergency.

Research current market prices for any product or service you are selling. Make sure to know the full range from high to low. Be aware of what competitors are charging for their products, and prepared to offer yours at a cheaper price. Talking about rivals is never good business; build up your own respect with your offers.

Make sure your home business respects local zoning laws and ordinances. If you do not, you could get shut down as well as fined and that can be embarrassing. Aside from reading and rereading laws to follow them, don't make enemies with anyone else. Keep a low profile. Sometimes this translates into limits on signs, as well as noise constraints. Do your best to remain unobtrusive.

Look for ways to get your business supplies wholesale. There are plenty of great Internet sources for all types of supplies. Many of which offer unbeatable deals. It is great to owning a certified business license. This will allows you to grab these products under exclusive prices and conditions.

The boundary between home and work often blurs when you live in both locations. Have a dedicated work space and work schedule. This will allow you to spend your nonworking time with family and friends.

To get the most business deductions when tax time rolls around, consult an accountant. Discuss these things before your business opening to better track the expenses for those write offs. Write-offs can lead to a lot of money saved over time so you want to take advantage of all that is available to you.

This book has provided you with trustworthy information. Which comes from those who run successful home based and brick/mortar businesses for many years. Running a business takes hard work, dedication and doing your homework first. If you put in the effort, you are more likely to see a reward. Continue learning, the more you learn the better your chance will be. In running a successful home-based business whether online or offline there are no short cuts.

Chapter 10

Profitability is one the key note in the chapter. Tips To Help You Run A Profitable Home Based Business Online and or Offline.

It seems like everyone wants to run a business from home, but most people aren't sure what they need to do to get started. If you're one of those lost people who doesn't know how to make your dream a reality, this book is for you. It is here to help. Read on for tips about running a work from home business.

It's healthy to take short breaks over the course of your work day. Don't use your break time to take care of complicated personal matters. For instance, don't do house chores or make personal calls. Take some time to recharge your batteries by taking a walk or sipping on a cup of tea.

Schedule your work hours, and stick to your plan to ensure that you also get adequate personal time.

You should select an ending time, and make sure that you stop receiving calls at that time. Be sure to schedule enough time for your loved ones and friends and for your own interests.

Join an online marketing business forum. There, you will be among others in your position of learning the ropes in home based business operations. Other people running home businesses know what kinds of challenges you face, and you can swap solutions.

The business name that you choose should be meaningful and important. Buy a domain name for your business, even if you haven't planned the site out. Domains are cheap so you need to grab one before another person does. You may want to post a site with only one page until you decide if you want a complete website or not. Site builders one page site are great for just a page your name and address and a brief description of what you are offering and some images. Use home business forums to get support from other home business owners. There are many online resources for those that own a home business enterprise. The information on these sites is valuable, you can always Google search your need. In the forums you can find people who are going through the same issues as you. You can share and learn from them as you navigate your way through the business world.

Establish an emergency fund to help stabilize your business with some financial security. Such a fund helps you deal with unplanned costs and maintain smooth operations. Especially during times of financial uncertainty. Only use this emergency fund when it is an emergency. Make it a top priority to replace this money.

It is vital that you keep accurate records for your work from home business. This is so you have all the documentation you need if the IRS or Revenue agency depending on where you are. If they decides to audit you, they will need you to provide the documentation. Maintaining complete documentation also facilitates better operation of the business.

Check how much you'll have to spend to start up your new home based business. Your costs may be lower than a traditional business, but they still need to account for every expense you made. Learn how much your business costs to operate so that you can be sure to turn a profit. By doing this from home you will gain added benefit to yourself. Beside basic necessity you will see you have most the expenses already in existence. That is what make a smart success strategy for you to start from your home.

Now you have strong resource to arm you with the knowledge necessary to get down to business. Remember that the material in this piece only works if applied. So use the information you read, and your business should be successful in no time and stay focused on your goal.

Chapter 11

In this chapter we are going to look into how and what you need to do to make Your Home Business Enterprise More Successful in today's marketing place.

Not much compares to the thrill of beginning a new work from home business owner. And who wouldn't enjoy the idea of working for themselves? When you are your own boss, though, you have an obligation to treat yourself as a professional and to get the most out of your business. You will learn a few great tips to run an effective home business enterprise whether online and or offline.

Try not to work straight through the day, as your body and mind needs some rest. For example, don't use your break to have a half-hour phone conversation with your family. Or start a complicated home repair or cleaning up at home. Take active breaks to refresh your body and mind, for example a bit of exercise or work in your garden. Take yourself away from the environment.

Mark products that aren't in stock so that people won't feel disappointed to find you don't have it anymore. Customers find it especially frustrating when orders they've placed not available. Will not fulfilled for several days, let alone weeks. Avoid selling products that are out of stock; if they are, inform your customers so that they are not left waiting while you restock. Offer your customers alternative at a discount if you are able to do a discount for the time being.

Do something that you love when you are starting a home business enterprise. A lot of people think that lessons from private people are better than school because the schedule isn't as rigid. Anything related to hobbies, like photography, art, or music, qualifies for home business environment.

Look for forums and social media community online to connect with people with like minds. This is a useful way to communicate with other entrepreneurs and also promote your enterprise. A single contact may help you reach new places that you didn't expect to reach so early; take advantage of each connection made online.

When working at home, office space is essential. Make sure that you will be comfortable in the space you choose. It should be somewhere you will be productive and efficient. It doesn't matter what size it is, you can do well in any space with the right planning.

A good way to gather information on running a home based business is join an online forum on the topic related your product and or service. Doing this will give you the opportunity to chat with other people in your position. You can all compare strategies, opinions and share your concerns.

To better track your business-related spending, open a specific checking account for your business. All your business transactions and expenses should put through your business account. This makes it easier to track your company's transactions. Also consider getting a credit card to use for business transactions, like ordering supplies.

Set daily goals and aspire to reach them. You may not get to everything every day, but goals can keep you working towards accomplishing what needs. Establish boundaries for a work from home business so that your family can respect what you are doing.

When you decide to own your home based business online and offline business by action. Tt is you who will handle all responsible for your failure or success. No need to look at that as a negative. Diligence pays off for people who operate their own businesses. Use the tips here that work for you and learn as you go. Soon you will have your own tips to pass onto someone else.

Chapter 12

When it comes to owning your own home based business. There are many tips and trick available to you. In this chapter we are going to cover Home Business Enterprise Tips That Anyone Can Follow.

Tons of information exists about launching and operating home businesses whether online or offline. You don't want to just buy anything. Read the tips in this book and the ones here in this chapter. Follow them to learn this is a genuine book about businesses in the home setting.

You have to be able to talk about your business to others. Keeping things simple and to the point will help to catch people's attention. Making your sound bite too long will lose the interest of potential customers.

At the launch of your business, send an email to your family, friends and co-workers that lets them know what you're up to. Offer discounts or freebies to your business get going. Encourage people to spread the news about your business. People who spread the word about your business to their friends can be helpful. Encourage the idea of spreading the news by giving incentives.

One marketing possibility is to use affiliates for your products. Swap affiliate links with fellow entrepreneurs as a way to boost everyone's business. This was also covered in the previous chapters as well. Become a part of a reliable affiliate program to promote similar products to yours. This is a great way to increase your income without having to do any hard work.

Ensure that your home based business online or offline starts off on the right foot by getting those closest to you on board. Managing a home business enterprise can be tough, a bit stressful and time consuming. But rewarding at the end of the day your goal to succeed should be your focus do what ever it takes to make it happen.

Your family must not only support you, but they must also allow you time alone for your work.

Pick a business that is likely to be profitable. Study the market for saturation. It is hard to turn profits when there is so much competition. Check out the prospective revenue of a home based business before you enter one.

Deposit all payments immediately. Make deposits every day, instead of every week. The less time a check lies around, the less likely you are to lose it. Make sure that you deposit via a bank teller instead of using the ATM. This way, you know that your money deposited without a problem.

You should be both honest and realistic about the expectations you have for your home based business. Are your products interesting, and do they capture the attention of potential buyers? Are you an upstanding person who values honesty?

It may be tempting to be lenient in finance with your customers as you start to build business relationships. But doing so may jeopardize your profitability. Make sure you set up payment terms that are clear for all your invoices and documents. Along with a reasonable penalty, like eight percent, over what the invoice amount is. If the total isn't paid within the normal payment terms.

Working alone from the comfort of your own home has its charms. But soon you will miss interacting with people in a face-to-face environment. Replace these office interactions by going out to other social locations on a regular basis.

Now that you've read this book, you will see that the tips here are not the kind of "secrets". Often the gurus reference to the secrets in their infomercials. The same methods used to run any other business. Also applies to running a home based business whether offline or online and with some useful tips, success can be yours. Remain plugged in the what is happening in your industry. Subscribe to newsletters in the same area of your business so you can stay informed on the trends as they come up.

Chapter 13

In this chapter we are going to look at some advice, if you are already in business you would wish you have heard sooner. Work From Home Business Advice You'll Wish You Heard Sooner! YES.

Most people have thought about being their own boss and running their own business. Perhaps it has been something your thinking about recently. Making your own work hours and not answering to a boss can be priceless benefits. If you need some ideas on running a home based business, continue reading this book.

You must go to any limit when you are working to make your customers satisfied. Pack a free gift with their purchases. Include a thank-you note expressing your appreciation for their business.

Two things that customers like are appreciation and free things. Make it known to your customer that you appreciate their business.

Join a couple of discussion groups, social media site and forums that discuss the topic of work from home business. If you search the internet, there are hundreds of sources of great information. There are lots of online articles and blogs that you can find to be useful.

Your business' name must have personal meaning. Even if you're not ready to host a business website, you need to get the domain name purchased. A lot of domains run under $10 per year; you want to secure yours before your competition does. Before you decide what your web site needs are. Post a small, one-page site that lists your products images. Contact information, business name and other important information.

To keep your tax bill low, track your business expenses. Expenses, such as Internet service, business mileage and office supplies. You should kept track of every expense and keep records. When you're a business owner, you can use many of your business-related expenses as tax deductions.

Even if it is just for a small amount, deduct them as well. Every penny counts.

Use a good business plan. Define your goals, resources and methods, no matter what size your business is. A well-thought out business plan will provide you with guidance. Will also help keep your business headed in the right direction as it grows.

Make your work from home business fit into your family schedule. If your business will make things difficult for your family, it may be time to consider alternative business ideas.

As soon as you receive payments, deposit them. Don't wait weeks or months to deposit payments; do it at least every few days. Deposit checks right away, so you do not lose them. When you do deposit it, go to a teller rather than using a ATM. This helps to ensure that the check gets deposited into your account.

Take the time to consider if your expectations are realistic. Do you have an outstanding product with long-term commercial potential? Do you have any experience running this type of business? Do you have what it takes to run it with the honesty and integrity that people expect from a business owner?

No matter the business you are looking to run from your home, the most important thing is to serve all your customers well. Being your own boss means you are responsible for managing your time and activities. Always be open to learning new things. Flexibility is a virtue for a businessperson. It won't be long before you will see the results you want for your home based business.

Chapter 14

Here are more tips! Take A Look At These Great Home Business Tips!

Starting your own home based business is both nerve-wracking and exciting. It can be difficult to get a good grasp on where to start. How can you become successful? You will have to establish a clear plan and make educated choices. This book I wrote just for people like you. It provides clear direction on how to run a work from home business both on line and off line.

You should prepare to give a sound bite that can explain your business. Cultivating the skill of being succinct when describing your business. You will impress possible new customers. This sound bite can also help you come up with ideas for a good company slogan.

Launching your home based business online and or off line is tough, but rewarding. One way to help ensure success is to find your own niche. That can be any topic you enjoy, but it is smart if it's something you know a bit about. Research your potential market as much as possible before you invest your energy and resources there. It is also a wise idea to network with other people who have a successful online business.

Wear business attire when working at home. Working at home sometimes makes you feel as if you can sit around in your pyjamas. As with any other job, you should dress for success. This helps you keep a productive mindset.

Again, Join forums and discussion groups for home businesses online or off line. Find communities in your area. As they say Networking is breakfast of champions. Besides chatting with others in your position, you can also create a name for yourself. Networking environment like this can often pay off!

When working at home, office space is essential. It does not have to be a large office, but it should be neat and organized well. Set up a room that inspires you to work hard and makes you feel comfortable and calm. Size is not as important, so make whatever area you have work.

It is important to invest in some business cards. Many online companies will make you business cards at little to no cost. These cards should contain basic information including your name, the name of your business. Include contact information such as phone number, website and email address. You should also list your email address and website. The more options your customer has, the more likely they will use one to contact you.

Record all the money you spend on your business, and you will have the opportunity to get money back at tax time. Expenses, such as Internet service, business mileage and office supplies. You should all track of every receipt. Being an owner and operator of your own business, your expenses have expenses of their own that you can removed off your taxes. Even if the amounts are small, it will save you money on your taxes.

As mentioned earlier in this book, a work from home business can be both appealing and intimidating. Reading this book have giving you gleaned some good information and advice from the tips shared in this book. Put that advice into action, and watch as things begin to work more for your work from home business.

Chapter 15

Now! Find Success In Home Based Business Without Losing Your Mind

Can you recall why you started your work from home business? You learned everything you could back then, didn't you? There is so much new data to learn! Get back into action with this book.

Dress for success. There is a great temptation to not dress well when working from home. Wear work-appropriate clothing just as if you were commuting. You can be as productive as possible if you keep a good head.

Take regular breaks throughout your day, but don't get distracted by the home environment. For instance, don't do house chores or make personal calls. Refresh your mind and body with active breaks like a short session of exercise or working in the garden.

Make your home office as comfortable as possible, and stock it with all necessary supplies. Although this is something that people saw as trivial. A lot of people just aren't efficient if their office doesn't work for them.

Keep family interruptions to small while working from home. Interruptions can corrode your productivity. So tell everyone when you will start working — and when you will done. Let them know you can work more and have more time to be with them if they respect your work time. Make sure your children have supervision and that they can reached you in an emergency.

Once again join forums about home business-related topics. This can be a good way to network and to establish a name for yourself, this is so important for your success. You could score the contract of a lifetime through doing this.

Keep track of what you are spending and earning by opening a separate account for your business. Make sure all business transactions use this account. This makes it easier to track your company's transactions. Also consider getting a credit card to use for business transactions, like ordering supplies.

Your business' name must have personal meaning to you and what your are promoting. Even if a business website is not yet planned out, buy that domain name as soon as possible. You can find a domain name for a reasonable price for a year. But make sure you buy your domain name before anyone knows about your business. You want to secure the name before giving out your information. If you haven't yet figured out if you want a sophisticated site. Put up a place-marker that has your contact information and name on it.

Having an instant page is a great idea at the beginning until you figure out your game plan for your domain.

If you want to save money, on your business expenditures you must documented for accuracy and tax purposes. This includes car mileage related to your business and internet service. You will find that many items are tax deductible when you own your own business. Be sure to keep track of all expenses, no matter how small, because they add up.

Make sure you follow all zoning laws and other applicable laws related to your business. If you don't, you might encounter fines, closures and embarrassment. Even if you follow all the regulations, you have to be sure that you keep a low profile. For example, keep signage tasteful and unobtrusive. Reduce traffic and noise. Try to be as courteous as possible.

Finally, you need the same fire in your belly that you had for your home business enterprise when it began. Success only comes to those who put the effort in. All this information in this book will guide you on getting started. You will find this book informative and will help you in your journey of owning your financial independence.

Chapter 16

In this chapter we touching topic that require a professional assistance. Tips And Tricks On Reducing Your Tax Bill For Your Home Based Business.

Having a home based business online and or off line can be just as intimidating as it is appealing. Where do you start? How are you going to do it all yourself? You need to address all your questions. There are many tips out there, including those in this book, that will guide you on making a work from home business successful.

If you need to "wine and dine" your clients, make sure that you deduct the cost of these meetings during tax time. Many of these types of meetings considered to be tax-deductible business expenses. Make sure that the people you meet with are either already clients or potential clients. As the IRS or tax agencies does not favour claiming regarded as pleasure as business expense.

Starting home businesses can be fun but challenging as well. Getting Started on a home business requires finding your niche market. It can be anything that people need or want and it helps if you know about the subject already. Research your potential market as much as possible before you invest your energy and resources there. Be certain to network whenever possible with other home business enterprise entrepreneurs.

Do you have an office? You do not need a lot of space but do your best to create an inviting office. An office needs to be where you're able to inspire, efficient and productive all at once. Don't concern yourself with the total size; you can work with any size space.

Starting a business-specific checking account. This will help you to establish a solid paper trail for your business transactions. Use your account for all deposits, payments and expenditures related to your business. This enables you to analyze all your company's financial transactions. Get a business credit card as well to use for related expenses.

Choose a business name that has some kind of personal meaning to you. Start by purchasing a domain name for your website. Many times you can get a domain for under $10 per year, but it is important to reserve your domain before another person takes it. When you are still trying to decide whether you need a full website, post a page that has all your business information on it.

As I mention instant pages are great for this reason, find a web hosting company that have instant pages.

You should start by determining how much setting up your work from home business will cost you. Home businesses do not cost as much as traditional businesses, but there will still be costs you will need to take into account. If you calculate your home business enterprise expenses, you can figure out how to reduce the chances of losing money.

Go on the internet and get things you need at your office at a good price. Luckily for you, the Internet is perfect for finding all the prices and requirements that you'll need. At startup a few things needed start collecting everything your will need. If this your first work from home business adventure take you need get what's needed. Use your business certificate or license to get these wholesale prices.

As mentioned earlier in this book, a home business can be both appealing and intimidating. You have gained some good information and advice from the tips shared in this book. Put that advice into action, and watch as things begin to work more for your home business enterprise.

As you move forward things will come up your way like how to find New Customers For Your Home Business

Using the Internet as a tool, you can dig up tons of information and secrets about any topic imaginable. Learning how to run a home-based business is easy to do by going online. This piece is part of the vast body of information that can help your home based business.

If you must take clients out, you can itemize these expenses. Meetings with business associates deemed legal business costs. Always make sure that you are only writing off meetings that are with actual clients. Or individuals that you are hoping will become clients. Because other meals and entertainment opportunities are not tax-deductible.

It can be both rewarding and frustrating to build a home based business online and or off line. You must first identify a niche for your business, this is important. Try to find something that you are good at and have knowledge in already. Put a lot of research into the process before investing with your resources. Also, network with those who've ran their own businesses to get ideas and tips.

If you are selling a product that you make, be sure that you know how much it is costing you to create, because you do not want to be losing money.

Wholesale sellers often offer their products at twice the cost to make them. Along those lines, your retail price would be two times your wholesale price. Make it a fair price both you and the customers can agree upon.

Joining a network of other online business owners can be beneficial to your success. It helps to build a network with other peers. It is not necessary to network with people selling the exact same item. But surrounding yourself with other motivated home based business owners is helpful.

Take the time to talk to a business attorney around your area before you start your home business. You want to make sure you understand local laws and regulations when working out of your home. The business lawyer will inform you about these laws. He can also walk you step by step through your set up to make sure you adhere to the laws.

Put together a quality website visitors will remember. Choosing a name for your domain that is too long or tough to spell means that your clients will forget it. Your domain name should be short and to the point.

Pick a business that is likely to be profitable. Examine the market for your business idea, and make sure it is not already saturated. It will be difficult to make much money if you have a lot of competitors. Do your research and find out which business is the best for you pay attention to the financial reward.

Create a work schedule. If you don't set office hours, you'll work all day and night. Let yourself have some free personal time and make up a schedule like one you would have if you worked at a company. You'll still have a social life later on if you do this.

You will get great results if you use the tips you just read. Reread this pages as often as you feel is necessary. Having the right information and knowing how to use it is the key to home business success.

Chapter 17

Want more Information On Home Business Enterprise? Keep reading these following chapters and more tip for you to Check Out.

Many people find it hard to comprehend how to start and run a home based business for obvious reasons. But, it doesn't need to be as difficult as you may first think. Understanding the process starts with learning, such as reading this book and the rest of the chapters below.

Save gas receipts and document mileage if your work from home business involves any driving while you are working.

These expenses help reduce your tax burden since they are 100% deductible. But, you must prove that that driving is essential to the profit of your business.

Keep a special business phone line to keep it separate from your personal phone line. A professional business always has a dedicated line and voice mail system. Not only that, but you don't want to risk your child or another person answering a business call on your behalf. Unless trained to do so, you can have a call centre answer your call when you are not able to answer.

Plan for periodic breaks when working from home. But don't allow yourself to become too preoccupied with what's going on in your household. Leave personal phone calls, chores, and errands for when your work day is over. Use your breaks to get much needed exercise and fresh air.

You will find forums online which have dedicated people like yourself. People running a work from home business like yourself. You will be able to connect with other online business operators. Other people running home businesses know what kinds of challenges you face, and you can swap solutions. This is a great way to learn from others in your line of business. "Networking is breakfast of champions".

Keep this in the back of your mind and be open to learn from others.

Knowledge is power! LEARN as you go.

You need to write a business goal, a description of your business done in just a couple sentences. Your statement should tell a bit about your business goals. Why you started the business and any other mission related information. You should be able to tell people what you are all about and why you stand out, be unique.

To get the most out of your business, make sure you are taking advantage of any and all deductions on your taxes that you can claim. You can save a lot on your taxes by claiming your entitle deductions.

If you wish to be successful when you have a home business, becoming comfortable at self-promotion. You have to be able to talk to anyone and everyone about what you do or sell. It is important that your customers find your business and its offerings to be of impeccable quality. You must be comfortable with self promotion if you want your business to be successful.

It is important to always look to the future. While you should celebrate each success as it happens, you have to put them in the past after the celebration. Keeping your focus on whatever is coming in the future is more important than past events. This will ensure that you prepared for all upcoming obstacles and are ready for any opportunities. In this manner, there will not surprises.

It is not hard to promote a business once you know what you are doing. Having a well-designed website is vital for just about any business, so think about setting one up. You can set up the website on your own within a day. Domain registration is sometimes free, but usually you'll need to pay a nominal fee. If you wish to make large profits, then you will not mind the fee in the slightest. Also you need to be in social media community and or start a community of your own and or a group. Invite your friends and business associates to your group and make it engaging with your product and or service

Remember everything you have read. Keep all these tips in mind and use them when you launch your home business. Trying some of these new tips is the best way to move toward success.

Chapter 18

When it come to starting any business the information available is endless. This chapter we are going to look at Home Based Business Information Everyone Should Take Advantage Of.

Between Internet articles to paid programs and news programs. There are so much information about having a home based business online and or off line. Be certain you don't buy any old things. This book is a must as far as reliable information goes, so read on.

Don't forget to deduct part of your Internet connection expense. You can write off the Internet costs, but if you use it as a home connection as well, you cannot claim more than 50% the cost on you taxes. Read the rules on the IRS website.

If you have to drive a lot for your business, make sure you watch your gas mileage and keep receipts for whatever gas you use. These expenses are 100% deductible when you do your taxes. It is important to keep close track of these records in case of auditors come to edit your files in the future.

Dress for work, as if your customers will see you. In a home office scenario, you may feel the desire to work in your pajamas. Instead, wear clothing that would be appropriate for an ordinary workday. This can improve focus and productivity.

Select a name for the business that is special to you. This can be the actual name of your business or domain name. The cost of a domain is quite low, and if you have one in mind you need to buy it before someone else snatches it up. You should create a simple page with your contact information and put it online while you develop your website.

Your family needs to be supportive of your online business. A online business will take up a lot of your time, and it can be hard and stressful work. Your family must not only support you, but they must also allow you time alone for your work.

Use the internet to buy home business enterprise supplies at wholesale prices. There are great sources online for locating the information and supplies you will need. For your venture to become a home business enterprise owner. To buy your supplies at wholesale you need a business license.

Always focus on what you want to happen next and plan for it. When you win at something you definitely should celebrate. But, you need to realize that this is success is over, and put you behind you once it's over. Your focus now needs to be on the upcoming days and weeks. Keeping your mind on the future will make it easier for you to know what you need to capitalize on, and what obstacles may be coming. That way, you won't blindsided by something you were not looking for.

Be sure to stay in touch with the customers of your home based business online and or off line. But don't overburden them with communication. If you update your content or offer lots of specials, let your customers have the option to sign up for emails or newsletters from you. Make sure you don't overstep your limits when it comes to communication.

You'll be a lot better informed after reading this piece. Yet, it may not be quite the information the self-proclaimed gurus want you to know. The fact remains that home businesses need the same discipline of all other businesses.

Chapter 19

Gaining Valuable Knowledge About Successful Home Businesses

Home businesses are growing at a rapid pace. Now it is easier than ever to follow your dream and become your own boss. There are more opportunities than ever before and there is a perfect one for you, too. This book can help put you on the path to your own home business success.

When running a business from home be sure to save every receipt from expenses incurred. For example mortgage, energy, insurance and phone payments. These expenses incurred in maintaining your home included in your deductible expenses. Add them when you are filing your taxes.

The percentage of your home used for the home business is the percentage of the expenses. That you can deduct from your taxable earnings. This is important for you, always consult with tax professional on issues related to filling your taxes. This will help you get a better clarification in Tax related expenses.

You need to think things through before investing in your decision when you are going to establish a home business. This careful thought will make sure that you are successful at it. You will not get yourself in over your head when beginning the home business venture.

I'm sure everyone has heard the saying "finish what you start." It is easy to realize that it's much harder to finish what you start than people think, as everyone gets older. Carrying out that dream takes hard work and determination, even though everyone can dream. Do not give up on your business. With your solid plan and a strong stomach, persevere!

Many home business owners tend to have health related issues because they get less exercise. Staying home and also overwork when the lines blur between work and life. At the same time, one of the major differences between being an employee at a company and running a home business is the lack of sick days. Because they run their own business, each day they might have to take off from getting sick translates into lost income. It is thus vital that home business owners take extra care of their health through exercise. Adequate sleep, and proper diets will help keep your healthy.

When you are trying to run your own home business, it is of utmost importance that you practice proper organization. When it comes to your paperwork and other related information. You must keep track of all financial papers and any other documentation that you have.

Often times, if this is not organized you can get yourself into trouble. Believe me this have happen to a lot of business owners. A lot of people learn the hard way don't be one of them.

As already discussed, home businesses are a big business these days. If you just open your eyes and keep on the lookout for the right one to come along, opportunities to be your own boss are everywhere. By implementing the advice in the book you may find success in a home business can be yours. Do it right the first time.

Chapter 20

If your home business online or offline keep reading. Building A Home Based Business Online? You Need To Read This!

Think about where you might be if you didn't have your home business enterprise. It either is the only income that you have, or it is a great supplement to the money you make otherwise. This book will give you ideas about how to grow your business into a prosperous enterprise.

You have to be able to talk about your business to others, self promote. You will have an easier time impressing potential clients if you can describe your business. Describe your business without being too wordy, keep it simple. These sentences should include the critical points of the business, giving you a starting point for a good slogan.

What else can you do if your business fails? You need contingency plans set in place for all kinds of mishaps. If you plan ahead, you will not end up in a rut while trying to fix things.

Building a business at home is fun, although challenging. First, you have to locate a niche for your home based business that agrees with you. It can be almost anything, but you need to understand it well. Do your homework before making a commitment to any one project. Network with other home based business owners to get an better idea of which sectors are the best.

Keep track of all manufacturing costs, such as materials, labor and time. For things like products which you produce, as doing so can prevent you from losing money. A wholesale mark-up from cost is approximately twice the base cost. If you are going to sell it at retail price, then multiply your wholesale price by two. Set your prices at a level that is fair for you, as well as your customers.

Do something that you love when you are starting a work from home business online and or off line. A lot of people think that lessons from private people are better than school because the schedule is not as rigid. Anything related to hobbies, like photography, art, or music, may taught in a home environment.

As you start your business, send emails to loved ones and co-workers about what you're doing. Offer a discount or free item to your first customers to jump start your business. Encourage people to spread the news about your business. There is nothing quite as effective as personal referrals.

Having a checking account designated for your business can help you keep track of your business spending. This was also mention in the previous chapters. Business expenses and orders should transacted using this account. It's the best and most accurate way to keep track of your business's activity.

For purchases like office supplies and miscellaneous expenses,

use a separate business credit card.

Identify your specific business niche again important, you want to be unique. Look for customers in wholesale and retail that want what you are selling. Once do this , making sales will become easier. Talk to anyone you know about what they think about your niche. Make sure to ask for referral business or offer incentives for referrals. Go to trade shows related to your industry and look at who is buying and what they are buying. Then, be sure to reach out to this audience.

In summary, having a home business is a big accomplishment. Making sure that it thrives will make you feel great and give you confidence. Hoped that you put the suggestions found here to good use and build a successful home based business to be proud of. Stay focus to your plan, your goal and never stop any thing to get there.

Chapter 21

A few things and reason for them. Why You Should Use A Work From Home Business Office.

While a home based business online and or off line might be appealing, it is also intimidating to some people. How do you get started? How will you make a profit? Most people have a ton of questions about how to get their home business started. As luck would have it, this book put together with you in mind.

You can get a tax deduction for your home business enterprise Internet costs. You will be able to deduct a percentage of your annual bill against your taxes. That percentage will be dependent if it used for personal use as well.

Be sure to keep your residential phone line and business phone line separate as mentioned in the other chapters. Looking professional is the best way to build a customer base. So having a separate number for your business and answer nice matter is key.

It can be both rewarding and frustrating to build a home based business online and or off line. Starting a home business enterprise requires finding your niche market. Pick an audience and a product you are already familiar with if possible you can always learn. You want to research as much as possible and expand. Instead of putting everything into one narrow-minded basket. Use networking events and tools to learn from others who have been successful. You want to connect with people who are creating a home business enterprise.

Feel free to have breaks during the day. But make sure you dedicate a chunk of your time to just work related things. Don't let the activities in your household distract you. For instance, don't do house chores or make personal calls. Take a physical and mental break by walking or just reading a great book for a while during your brake time.

Setting regular work hours for yourself and following them. This will help you maintain a good work/home life balance. Determine when business hours will end. Try not to work or accept calls after hours. It is important to set aside time for yourself, your family, and your friends.

Don't quit your job when you're just starting your work from home business. It may take awhile to make any money, so do not give up your day job. You will need to have money when you are waiting for your business profits to come in.

If you are artistic inclined, you could establish a business in which you provide graphic design services. To clients in the your area. Lots of enterprises prefer independent vendors over large firms. Because they can receive more attention and get better service. This you can used to your advantage.

One of the most important considerations when you are running a business from your home. Is to make the most of deductions you allowed to claim for the business. You can save a lot on your taxes by claiming your entitle deductions. Contact your tax professional about tax to be better informed. The repercussion for errors made are expensive can be damaging.

You should always look toward the future. It is important to celebrate past successes, but they have already happened. Keep your eyes on the goals you have set for today and the coming weeks. This will ensure and prepared you for all oth the upcoming obstacles and opportunities. This will, in essence, keep you from unexpected surprises.

As mentioned earlier in this book, a home business enterprise can be both appealing and intimidating. If this is your first time take care to make good decision. You have gained some good information and advice from the tips shared in this book and continue to learn more. Put these advice into action. Watch as things begin to work more better for your home based business online and or off line.

Chapter 22

Now you have started and things are running smoothly. In the chapter we are going to review Solid Ways To Improve Your Home Business Enterprise Revenue.

You may have many challenges at the start of your home based business. If you wish to have a company that's home based, you should use the things you have learn in this book. More of what you are about to learn in this last chapters will enlighten your understanding.

If your business requires lots of driving, be certain to keep gas and mileage records and track you distance. These travel expenses, even if they are only for a day trip is considered to be 100% deductible. You need to be able to prove that what you did while driving increased your business' profits.

The same applies if you have a travel business most of your travel is business related because of the nature of the business. Again seek the advice of your tax professional to clarify these areas and make sure you are in the right track.

Running a successful home based business online and or off line takes initiative and a drive to succeed. If you are going to run your business from your home, consider having or building a room dedicated to your business. A separate office and keep it professional office space. Some countries have laws about office space, so be aware of these when you make your decision.

Setting aside a dedicated space for your home office will keep you focused on your work.

Set a clear work schedule for yourself and use it to separate your home life from your business life, this is important. It is easy to mix things up if you are not careful. Pick a time of day when after which you'll no longer accept a business call. Allow plenty of time to spend with your family and friends, as well as time to relax and pursue your interests. Exercise for mental clarity, is important for your well being.

When you work from home, limit your family interruptions by all means. Interruptions are distracting, and distraction will impede your productivity. Let your folks know when you will be available. It is important that they understand that you need privacy. Let them allow you to spend time with them just as soon as you complete your work. Also, you will need to have someone babysit your children during working hours. If your kids are in school even better use those hours well to get things done.

Endeavor to be your best while working from your home office. Having a home business enterprise can be fulfilling, but your self-esteem can take a real hit if you put work before yourself. Take a shower each morning, limit snacks, and take time to get regular exercise.

Your self-esteem will always be important, no matter where you work. So maintain that high image you have always set for yourself.

If you find yourself intrigued about home businesses but do not know your potential niche yet, use the Internet to get some ideas. Know that there are tons of home based business scams online so be watchful of those scams and stay away from them. Always do your due diligence . Some scammers sell you things that you can find for free, such as government resources.

Some business ideas are just pyramid schemes, looking for an uninformed sucker. There are more complicated scams also which try to have you pay some fee to have access. To high income work that does not exist, or pay for online classes which are useless. Doing research will keep you from falling victim to something that is not legit.

Use a name for your business that is meaningful to you. If your business website is still just an idea, get your domain name registered. The cost of getting of domains is reasonable. You want to secure yours before your competition does. While working on the full website, put up a one page micro-site up. Includes your business logo, name, and contact information.

As before discussed, people attracted to being the own boss have to be willing to do what it takes. It will allow them to do what they want to do. By making use of these information, anyone can take steps to ensure that their home based business succeeds.

Chapter 23

How To Maintain A Professional Image For Your Work From Home Business

Take a moment to think about what your life would be like without the business you run from home. It may provide all your income need, or it may just supplement your wages. The following advice will help you make sure that your business remains successful.

Always put your customers' needs first, and go out of your way to please them. Try to do something more for you customer by including a thank you note or a small extra item in their package. This will show them that you value them as a customer. Clients love receiving free merchandise, and feeling appreciated by businesses they have relationships with. Show your customers that, that you're taking their business to heart.

If you want to be successful at running a home based business, you must take initiative and have the drive to succeed. Since many regulations apply to buildings and businesses. Check with your county to make sure the set-up you have in mind for your home based business doesn't create any legal conflict. You may find a separate office building on your property to be most suitable or create a space at your home. It can also be a great way to keep home life separated from your business life!

Do you have an office with the needed supplies that you feel comfortable in? This is a question you should ask yourself. A space that is free of distractions allows you to work more better.

Look for price ranges for a product in today's market before you start trying to sell. Set your prices based off competitor evaluations so you can be competitive in your offering. If you offer a comparison between yourself and the competition. But, highlight your good points rather than their bad points.

Reward customers who refer friends to your home business. One of the best ways to promote your business is by word of mouth. When people hear about a product or service from someone they know, they're more apt to buy over a flier they will throw out. Besides, incentives encourage customer loyalty.

Write down the daily goals that you have. There will be things you cannot get done, but you should be sure to set goals that you're able to reach. Set boundaries to work at home so that family can respect your work time.

Use the support available through forums on the Internet for people who work from home. You will learn that there are many online places to meet up with other home business owners. Other business owners are more than happy to share with you things and ideas they've tried. Whether those things and idea have brought success or not it is a learning process. When you hit a rough spot, this information can make a big difference for you so refer to this book.

When starting a home business you need to factor in how much available money you have for start up costs. Home businesses are cheap compared to traditional businesses, but "cheap" doesn't mean "free." Learning exactly how much money it will take to keep your business running will keep you from losing money later on.

Whether you have an existing home business enterprise or are thinking of starting one. These information are important to help you either way. You should make the most you can from your business. We hope that the advice you have found here will help you maximize your business now and in the future. If you have Questions About Home Business Enterprise Then Here Are Answers!

Your home business enterprise is like to a home, in which it requires a blueprint, a solid foundation. Lots of help and materials to put it together. The following book outlines critical elements of a business. A plan that will help guide you to success in your home based business.

Describe your business in a nutshell. You will have an easier time impressing potential clients. If you can describe your business without being too wordy that will help your in more ways than you can imagine. Within this sound bite is also the base for your business slogan. After all, everything important about the business is in the sound bite.

You should always be willing to take extra steps to leave your customers with a positive impression. Try including an unexpected free gift with their orders. Like a thank you card with purchases or anything else that shows them how much you value their business. Customers want to feel appreciated, and they also enjoy getting a free something. Make it known to your customer that you appreciate their business.

Have a banner page on your site. You can trade links or graphics with other websites, which have content on the same topic as yours. This is a great and easy way to improve your rankings in the search engines and will gain you more traffic.

Select a name for your business that is meaningful. Buy a domain name for your business, even if you haven't planned the site out. Domains can cost under $10 a year, and it is important to get one that is relevant to your business before someone else does. I stress this out quite often in the book for a reason. Once the name you want is gone you can not get back. If the person who registered the name want to give it up will not be cheap to get. If you haven't yet figured out if you want a sophisticated site that is ok. Just put up a place-marker that has your contact information and name on it for the mean time until you are ready.

Create a rigid schedule for work. If you don't set a schedule, you may end up working around the clock. Give yourself some free time and create a schedule like you are working for a large company. By doing this you will manage to maintain a social life.

Always save receipts if you work for your business through home or off your home. As a business owner, any expenditure that you have that relate to your business activities are tax deductible. Including the cost of transportation. Save all receipts associated with these expenses, as a lot of them will end up being deductible. You do not want to have any unneeded tax liability.

Register your company by setting up a DBA license. Your bank or chamber of commerce will be able to assist you with advice in this regard. It will not cost a lot of money and can isolate your business from anything personal.

If you are attempting to decide what product you want to sell or service you want to offer. Choose something that would make your life a little easier. Make sure that there is people interest purchasing the items. Something that will resolve an issue that they face on a daily basis. A successful product will solve a common, widespread problem.

Combine this with some advice from those who have gone before you, and your dream of owning a home business can become a reality. Building up your business takes a lot of hard work and dedication, and following the advice from this book will help you to get there.

Chapter 24

Though we have covered a lot of information on these chapters there are some tips you should not miss out in. Home Business Tips You Shouldn't Miss Out On

Many people want to start a business at home, but they do not know the proper steps or what they want to start their business on. If you fall into that category and don't know where to start, or how to start, by know you will know you have come to the right place. This book is full of great tips and information on starting and maintaining your business and building success.

Pay attention to all relevant local laws and ordinances. Neighbours could complain if the noise levels are too high.

If you use chemicals for your business, check about that as well. You want good neighbour relations through keeping a low profile. That means little traffic and discreet signage. Don't draw too much attention to yourself and your business.

Artistic talent means that you could sell graphic designs to area businesses. Designing for businesses is profitable, especially if you have the skills. Don't overlook this competitive advantage.

You should always have a good business plan for your home business. It's possible that you'll make alterations to this plan as time passes, and you may wind up throwing it out completely. No matter what, a business plan is essential for keeping your business, and you, on track. Focus on the goals you want your business to reach. You should rehearse your game plan every once in awhile. If you see it shifting to a different direction don't panic follow the trend. Sometimes the idea we start up with is not always what come out in real life practice.

To have a successful work from home business, you need to feel confident when promoting yourself. As a work from home business owner, you need to be able to represent your business to customers. Stressing the high quality of your products is essential in attracting your customers. You must know how to promote your business if you want to achieve serious success.

Having a website for promoting and selling your products is essential. When you run a home based business online and or off line you need an information site. Especially at the beginning until you decide on your plan for a website . You will increase your sales this way because your audience will be larger. So having a functioning site is idea. If your budget permits, professional website designers can produce quality websites for you. That could be better for you at the beginning without the challenges of creating your own website.

Ensure your work from home business won't interfere with your family routine. If you believe that the business will have a negative impact on family life, it may be wise to reconsider.

Have a clear understanding of what the goal is for your business. A solid business goal should offer a short description of the business practices and goals of your company. If you create an goal, you will have an answer ready when someone asks you to describe your business. This will be impressive to potential customers. Because it will show your confidence and knowledge.

Set a schedule to work. With set office hours, you will avoid working at all hours of the day and night, that can be tempting but don't fall for it. Pencil in some personal time, and keep your working hours reasonable. You will be able to hold onto your social life if you do this.

This book has given you some ideas about starting your home based business. Running your own business can be one of the most rewarding adventures of your life. But, you need to use these information if you want it to work out for you. Make an effort do that, and your business will be successful.

With all these set up plans and goals. Look for Great Tips For Achievement In Your Home Business goals.

From online articles to magazine to paid and special programs. There are ton of home business information out there so feel free to dig into them. Do not pay for every resource you find. The following book will help you to understand the reality of what it takes to run a home based business online and or off line.

Don't forget to deduct part of your Internet connection expense. Keep in mind that the percentage that you deduct from your bottom line can only be what used. Only what you use for your business and not for other uses. Be sure to contact you tax professional on these as well.

Make it a point to keep current and repeat customers satisfied with your business. Offer incentives to encourage more purchases and refer their friends. If your customers are happy, you will generate a lot of return sales. Happy customers will keep coming back for more.

When picking a product consider items that interest you, things you can use in your own life. If you are trying to decide what product to sell this will be idea for you in selecting a product. For a product to sell, it must fill a need consumers have that is not currently met. Consider your own needs when trying to determine the needs of your consumers.

Keep everyone informed when you are planning to start a business. Offer freebies or price breaks as a way to get the business going. Ask them to promote your business with others they know and give them incentive for doing so. Word of mouth advertising doesn't cost you anything and it can be effective.

Joining a network of other home business owners can be beneficial to your success. This was also mentioned in the previous chapters. You can find others to enlarge your own network. These people don't need to be in your same industry. But they need to be positive, supportive and understand. The unique challenges home business owners face daily can be demanding. Being in association of other can be of a great help for a new comer. These networks and associates can help you depending on what you need is and what kind of network you join.

Offer incentives to customers who refer others to you. Using word of mouth to advertise is the best advertising method. As a friend's recommendation carries more weight than a printed ad or any other kind of ads. This will encourage all your current customers to stay loyal.

Invest in professional looking, quality business cards. You can find business card offers online for free or cheap. Your business card needs to include the important contact data, like your name. Your company name, phone number and email address. It is important to include your email and website as well. Having all this information will make it much easier for customers and clients to contact your business. This will make some people feel more comfortable dealing with you and your company. Be open in giving our your contact for business related connections.

Create a fund for emergencies to help guard your business's financial well-being. You will be able to pay for any surprise expenses that may come up. With an emergency fund, which will assure your business continues to run in the miss of any unexpected out comes. Don't "borrow" from the emergency fund or use it for non-emergencies, and if you do use funds, replace them as soon as you can.

You should always save some of the money that you make in a year so that you can your pay taxes. Taxes usually run somewhere around 15% to 20% of your income verify this data with your tax professional. Setting aside a part prevents unnecessary scrambling at the end of the year to meet your obligations.

This book contains a lot of interesting tricks and hints about how to run a home business. Other well known writers haven't talked about some of these point yet. The same methods used to run any other business apply to running a home based business and with some useful tips, success can be yours. Set your goal and be determined to achieve it, don't let any thing discourage you in achieving your goal. Once again stay focused.

Chapter 25

Make Your Work From Home Business Profitable And Successful

Are you setting up a home based business? that is a question you need to think about. It will help you control your life and do work that is satisfying and enjoyable. It is still a genuine business, though. The more you know about successful business practices, the better of a position you'll be in.

To make your home-business venture profitable, you need ingenuity and ambition. There are regulations that specify what kind of building an office location. So keep this in mind when finding somewhere to host a business if that is what you wish to do. But, hosting at your home will be the best idea at the beginning. Consider renting office space, so you can separate home and work life, if you want to go that route.

The option is open to you depending on your budget and plan and the product and or service you are offering.

Before you try selling, you need to understand the price range in the market for the items you want to sell and or service you are offering. Look at the prices of comparable products, and aim to undercut the competition. While looking at competition, always maintain civility. You do not want to tarnish your own reputation by speaking ill of others. You can point out why you provide superior options instead this why you need to be unique in every way. You want to stand out and ahead of the competition.

It is advisable to be brief when writing the goal of your business. Think about why you created this business and what you wish to achieve. In these sentences, you should describe the exceptional qualities of your business and what you hope to do.

Always write up a business plan and edit it as time goes on, take it from me your business will change over time. You may have a small business, but you will always have goals. You need to figure out what you need to do to reach your goals short or long term goals. Planning out what you will do will give you the right framework to build your business.

If you are not good at self-promotion, you will struggle with your business at home. You need to learn how to talk about your business and get others interested in what you are trying to sell. Your customers need to feel your products are high quality. Self promotion is something you will need to learn how to do if you are going to bring in top profits.

Promote your work from home business as often as possible.

When you make small talk with people, you should mention your business if the conversation allows it. It's vital that you carry business cards with you at all times. So that you have them on hand to pass out during these types of occasions that warrants it. But, don't be spreading your business card to anyone in any event. The mood has to be right, the timing makes a huge difference or give out your business card when called for in a conversation.

Enough help is important in any business, especially a home-based business. If you are short-staffed, it can be difficult to get the kids to eat or take a nap. Get a day care that will fit your schedule will be helpful if you need such services.

Open a customer phone line for your home based business online and or off line. Such an expense is deductible in your business taxes. Or, you can keep records of what business calls you make so you can deduct a percentage of your phone costs. This is an option but it always a good idea to have a dedicated line just for your business.

Never take deductions that you can't justify at tax time. Track your expenses and earnings and do not wait until the last minute to put together a list of deductible items. Don't claim anything you use with your house instead of the business.

The ideas offered along these pages may prove beneficial when starting a home based business. Running your home business will be smoother with the right preparation. Do it well and your business should soon run like a well-oiled machine.

Chapter 26

How To Find Ideas For An Internet Marketing for Home Business

The thought of running a home based business for many people is intimidating and appealing. It can be hard to decide exactly what it is you need to start on, how and where to begin. You may also wonder how you will make it all workout for you. First, deal with these questions before getting started. With the following chapters at your disposal, some direction is at your fingertips.

Starting a home business can be exciting, but it also takes a ton of initiative and a burning desire to bring your dreams into reality. If you have the land, consider building an office space on your property just and option. This is beneficial in the sense that you will not have customers entering your personal space. The local government may have stipulations requiring it. This also helps you keep the spheres of business and home from intersecting.

It's important that you have an office with all the supplies you will need. A space that is free of distractions allows you to work more.

Pick out a business name in which you find some personal meaning is important. Regardless of whether you have plans to set up your website yet, you should still buy the domain name immediately. Before you start promoting or doing anything to reserve the name and or at list make sure the name is available. There are a lot of domains that cost no more than $10 a year, and you need to grab them before someone gets to them. This might sound rushed, it is better to secure your name. When you are still trying to decide whether you need a full website, post a page that has all your business information on it.

Make sure your work environment is a safe one. Include a fire extinguisher in the room and a smoke detector nearby. A computer that designed for your business' needs can make a big difference. The right type of fire protection helps you lower your business insurance costs. An ergonomic keyboard helps protect your hands if your are typing a lot and a way to prevent any issue with your wrist.

The name you choose should mean something to you and represent your business. Your name should be representative of what you sell, which is why it is important to have a name that customers can appreciate. A name that is easy to remember will be ideal for your business. Attach a quirky or inspirational story to your brand. These associations can set your brand down the path to success and build brand loyalty.

Although some of the perks of working at home, like wearing comfortable clothes can seem fun. You might miss speaking with people on a regular basis, like you did in a prior job. Make sure to get out, go to other locations. Involve yourself with others to maintain your personal interactions.

It's easy to immerse yourself within work when you work from home. Set aside time each day that devoted to your social life and your family, not working.

It's important to have insurance when you have a work from home business. This is vital if you'll be having customers visit your home. You want some protection in the event that someone has an accident on the property.

As mentioned earlier in this book, a home based business can be both appealing and intimidating. You have gleaned some good information and advice from the tips shared in this book. Put that advice into action, and watch as things begin to workout more for your home business enterprise.

Stay focused take baby steps don't leave any stone unturned. Always be learning, Knowledge is power your income grows with it.

Chapter 27

Great Home Business Enterprise Strategies That Anyone Can Use

Home based business ownership has a lot of benefits, such as choosing your hours and managing yourself. You also have the ability to run an enterprise in which you believe in. Read on for useful information on running a sound work from home business and generating the rewards you desire.

Take some breaks during the day, but don't get trapped by your television or other distractions. Don't call people up or get involved in a big home project. This will take you away from your business. Refresh your mind and body with active breaks like a short session of exercise or working in the garden.

Select a name for your business that is meaningful to you and your company product. This is important that is why it is express in almost all the chapters. Business domains are inexpensive, and you don't want to miss out on getting the website name that you want. Lots of domains are under ten dollars a year, and you need to get yours before others do important. If you have a name in mind secure it or at list check and make sure it is available. If it is just put up one page for now until you decide if you want to expand to a full website. That way you will secure you name while you prepare your business.

Make sure you keep records of all business expenses as this can help you save money at the end of the year. This includes things like business related car mileage and Internet service. Most of the expenses of running your business are tax deductible for business owners. Even if it is just for a small amount, deduct them as well. Every penny counts.

Plan every aspect of your home business enterprise. Your business plan may change a little or a great deal over time. This plan will act like a to-do list so that you can see your business goals and a path to meeting them. A plan will keep on tract and will show the direction your business is going. Your business plan should be evolving, and it will keep you in the right direction.

One of the best ways to ensure that your home business makes as much money as possible. Is to market your business and products on the internet and other ad soure. You can market your business online by blogging, writing articles, or sending out an email newsletter. These actions will increase the traffic to your site and can lead to greater success.

Always research the target market, your business will focus on. Though you may be well versed in your services and products. Knowing what your market is and where their needs lie, will help you create the right sales and marketing plan. Right sales and marketing plan will bring visitors and customers to your site. When you design your website, keep in mind how customers usually buy your product or service. Find a tracking system that will help you watch the traffic source. Tracking will help you target your advertisement.

There may be unwritten rules you do not know about.

When creating a domain name, make it easy to remember and catchy. If you pick a domain name which is hard for people to spell or remember, people are less likely to visit your site. Interesting and simple is the best choice for domain names.

Operating your own home based business need not be arduous. Have a plan and stick to it; you will soon see the advantages of working out of your home. It is a great feeling to be able to work for yourself and set your own hours. Keep these tips in mind and build your business! Continue to run your own Home Business Enterprise with these tips. Before starting your work from home business, it is important to get information from as many sources as possible. Make sure you don't buy just anything that's available. Read and reread these tips to see how to run a home business.

If you are having to drive all over the place when you're working from home. Make sure you keep track of the miles you travel and the price you pay for gas as well. Such expenses are tax deductible, no matter how long or short the trip. But, make sure you can prove that the driving is necessary to the business' profit.

It's healthy and recommended to take short breaks over the course of your work day. Don't use your break time to take care of complicated personal matters. But, you should not let your personal issues take away from your home business enterprise. Rejuvenate yourself with regular breaks and physical exercise.

If you plan to hire any worker do a background and previous work history check on them. Recommended if you are think of hiring for your home business enterprise. Family members are often the first choices if you have that option. Poor employees can turn a successful fledgling business into a flop. So be sure that you hire reliable people with the skills needed to help your company grow.

Join forums about home business-related topics, social media groups. Not only is this a great way to network with like-minded professionals. But it is another way to get your name and product out there to others. Someone you meet there could help you build your profits. Just by sharing ideas and information could lead you to great resources you would not have had access to, so connect.

If you want a work from home business. But, don't know what kind of business you'd like to start yet. The Internet can give you plenty of ideas that are successful. Know that there are tons of home business enterprise scams online, don't over look anything in the process.

There are a lot of places that will offer you basic information that you can found elsewhere for free. The information have to be usable. Because if it doesn't tell you anything you don't know it is worthless. There are trickier scams which try to lure you into paying money to get a chance to do allegedly lucrative work that does not exist. As you have heard many times, if something sounds awesome, then it is likely to be a scam. If it is too good to be true it often not true.

Make sure that you are not breaking any laws or ordinances in your area. If you don't, you could find yourself facing fines and possible shutdown of your business. Do everything to the letter of the law, and try to keep your relationship good with your neighbours by staying low-key. That means little traffic and discreet signage. Stay invisible.

Supplies for your business can procured at remarkable discounts online. Internet searches can turn up tons of suppliers who will sell you any type of supplies. You would need supplies for your home based business. Shop online and keep your cost at low. Look for cost-effective prices. Having a business license will give you the power to buy supplies at wholesale look into getting one.

Big money in home business comes from experimenting and taking risks. Envisioning fresh and creative ideas and putting them to the test. This can result in a larger customer base, and a significant increase in sales and profits. If you let yourself fall into a routine, you may miss a lot of new opportunities that come up.

Now that you have read this piece, you may have noticed that the advice is straightforward. Home businesses use the same principles and foundations as other regular businesses. So don't be mislead by high priced courses that promises so much and delivers little or nothing to your success.

Chapter 28

Try This Advice To Work For Yourself With Your Own Home Business

There is no need to leave your home to start up and maintain a home based business. This can only work if you are aware of how to start a business and run it well. You have learned some great advice right here from this book.

Operating a home based business allows you a lot of benefit in tax deduction that can help your business. Some example

if you often entertain clients with dining out or other activities. Keep in mind those kind of expenses are tax deductible expenses. Done from your taxable income, to get more details on what your entitled to, contact a tax professional for details. These meetings should be legitimate expenses for your business. Make sure that any of the expenses that you deduct in this way are due to meeting current or potential clients. This is to make sure that the deductions are legit.

Have a quick summary of what your business does ready at all times. Cultivating the skill of being succinct when describing your business. That will impress possible new customers. You can even shorten it into a slogan!

Do your absolute best to keep up with your personal needs when working at home. You can get a lot of pleasure from running a work from home business. But you should not put it before yourself or your self-esteem can suffer. Shower every morning, get your regular exercise and keep snacking limited.

Your self-esteem will always be important, no matter where you work. So maintain that high image you have always set for yourself.

Do you have an office or have you considered an office, do you need and office? You do not need a lot of space but do your best to create an inviting office. An office must be quiet, organized and inspiring. Don't concerned about size as you can do well with whatever sized space you have.

Make sure you have a separate business account so there are records of business transactions. Make sure all business transactions use this account. You'll have an easier time keeping track of your income and spending, as well as being able to spot any fraudulent activity. Try to get separate credit cards that you can use for business transactions.

If you're an artistic person, you may be able to create a business that sells graphic designs. Many times local business prefers working with independent designers instead of a large companies. Because of the flexibility and individualized service available from independents. That's one place where you have a great advantage over larger companies. This is an option in considering your own home based business.

Make sure that your website has flair and is not mundane. Don't choose something long or hard to spell. Catchy and easy to remember are the things you must work towards when choosing a domain name for your business.

Determine the prices of your products. If you will be producing your own product, find out what it will cost to make it, it is service how long it will take you to complete. A rule-of-thumb standard says that to price a product, it should be set at twice what the merchandise costs to produce. That is what dictates what price to charge others for your wholesale products. You should multiply your wholesale prices by three for an appropriate retail price.

As mentioned, a home business enterprise is a great source of income for you, if you have the right tools and information. These tips will help you build a business with endless possibilities.

Here are some hints and helpful Ideas for the Home Business Enterprise Owner. A lot of people today are finding the potential of creating and operating a work from home business. But, there is a great deal of competition among home businesses. Thus, you need to educate yourself to succeed you may have heard the phrase knowledge is power. This way you will be able to lead the pack.

It is important to dress for success as I before mention, even if you are just working out of your home. If you work from a home office, it is tempting to stay in your pajamas all day. Instead, wear clothing that would be appropriate for an ordinary workday. Wearing real clothes affects not only your appearance, but your motivation to get down to business.

If you don't know what you want to sell, think about what products you want or need. This I need to stress out a bit more because a lot of people have issues deciding on the product to offer. Figuring out what consumers need is the most important step in choosing a product to sell. If there is a product that would solve a problem in your life, it would be helpful to others as well.

One good way to make money at home is by offering lessons in something that you know how to do. You can offer a flexible schedule, and offering this to your clients allows them to avoid the rigid schedules of schools. You can teach piano or guitar, or hobbies like knitting. Maybe you are a sharp photographer. Teaching can make you money, it is a service no overhead cost to you.

When you start a home business, seek out people who will support you. This support network is something your will have to build up yourself. While those in your group might not work in your specific industry. But, you will have the common bond of owning a home based business online and or off line.

Get involved with a home based business online community. You will be able to connect with other home business enterprise operators. Other people running home businesses know what kinds of challenges you face. You can swap solutions to help each other in any way you can.

The internet is a great source of information on the types of business available. Including their potential profitability. Know that there are tons of home business enterprise scams online as well so don't over look anything. If someone is selling information you can get for free by a simple online search, avoid it. There are those tricky scams as well that take your money for various things. As you have heard many times, if something sounds awesome, then it is likely to be a scam watch out for those.

Online forums can link you up with other business owners who can help you. There is a huge number and variety of sites and forums for work from home business owners. The support and understanding is invaluable. The more experienced members of these forums will mentor beginners. At the same time offer invaluable business advice.

Affiliates can help a lot when starting a work from home business. Connect with other owners of home businesses to trade affiliate links. Find out about successful, existing affiliate programs. Just to see if the products they promote complement your own. You can boost your revenues without the need to increase your inventory, drop shipping ideas will be great for you. You do not want to tie up your capital in inventory at the early stage of you business.

Applying these information should help you keep your business running well. You always need to be up to date with your knowledge, to keep your business going and ensure you are doing everything to succeed. Find out what you can do and build up strategies that you're able to use to be successful.

Chapter 29

Easy Solutions to Running a Business At Home

Sometimes life can throw you curve balls. You may lose your job after working for many years, and you may be unsure of what to do. Did you ever think about working from home? The advice in this book can be a springboard to getting you started.

If it's required that you use your vehicle to perform work-related responsibilities. Track the amount of miles you travel and save your receipts from the gas. These expenses help reduce your tax burden since they are 100% deductible. Prove this and you will save a lot of money during the year from running your home based Business.

Starting home businesses can be fun but challenging as well. Deciding on your own niche is the first and most important step of running your own home based business. Your niche can be anything, though it helps if you are familiar with the subject first. Spend enough time researching your niche before you get started. Network with others who are successful in working from home business owners.

Consider starting a membership with an online forum and or social media groups. This will put you in the position to get great ideas and advice for your home business enterprise. You can search out some good ones and get useful information from them. Blogs are another great resource when it comes to educating yourself about online businesses. Creating a great content through blogging is always a great idea to start on. There are so many free blogging platform you can get account on.

Don't expect your home business enterprise to be successful if you don't have the drive to take the initiative and make it work. You may want to build your own home office that your customers can enter, since many countries have office regulations. This will allow you to save money that you would have spent on paying for office space to rent. Plus you'll also save on gas since you won't need to make a daily commute if you operate from home.

Do you have an office with the needed supplies that you feel comfortable in? It may not seem important, but it's hard to work when you don't have the supplies you need and a comfortable space to work in.

Generate a good mailing list for clients. Make sure that your communications stay beneath the level of spam. One common use of mailing lists is to tell customers about new products and promotions. They also allow you to send out information, such as press releases or testimonials, or even coupons. Let people sign up for your mailing list on your website, blog and or fan page.

Make certain to search for home business supplies online to see if you can get them at wholesale cost. Online shopping will reveal a mass amount of product with competitive pricing for the sale of this kind of product. Owning a certified business license will be helpful. This will allows you to grab these products under exclusive prices and conditions more savings for you.

While reading this book, you're inspired to take your life into your own hands. You have received a lot of tips about starting a home based business online and or off line. Now is the time to grab the bull by the horns and go for it! You can keep this book for reference to read anytime you are not sure what the next step you should be taking for you business.

Trying These Tips For Successful Home Business adventures. As we know home businesses aren't simple to run, so people say. Many feel that the income is not stable enough and that any home business online or off line job is only meant as a part-time band aid. In these chapter we have discuss in details some solid advice for achieving optimal success. But the work and determination to succeed has to come from you. In the field of home based business it is never easy but, if you're determined you will get to where you need to be.

You must dedicated to have a successful home business, it is not easy but it is doable. You may want to consider renting or building an office for your business if you have the option to do so. This would be helpful if you will have face to face contact with customers. This is also an excellent way to maintain appropriate and clear boundaries between work and home.

Having a dedicated office space is an important part of any home based business. It may seem silly, but if you are not comfortable and have all you need, you may not be productive.

Keep colleagues, family and friends informed of your launched business with a simple email. Again as mentioned in the other chapters offer freebies or price breaks as a way to get the business going. Enlist their help in getting the word out about your business. People trust the referrals of their friends and family and it is important to apply this to your new venture. If your friends and family do not know anything about your business or even about you starting one. It will be hard for them to refer people to your business. Keep information flow open with you closes friends and family even though they may not like the idea but it is worth trying out. It is hare to predict their reaction with out trying out by giving them the proper information about you business.

Discussion groups are available online that filled with professionals running businesses from home. This can be a good way to network and to establish a name for yourself. You can never tell where your next profitable contact will come from, so take advantage of every opportunity. Take control every opportunity that come your way and make it work for you when it comes around.

Every work from home business should have a solid business plan. This idea of having a business plan I emphasize a lot in this book. Reason being that it is like having a road map to a journey. A journey you have not had before. The only way to find your way it to have a plan to where you are going. A plan will guide you through the part. Even small home businesses need to have delineated goals. A good picture of any needed resources and some strategies for meeting the goals. Having a plan in place will help you stay on top as your business grows.

Any home based business online and or off line should use all the tax deductions that are applicable to their situation. You can save a lot on your taxes by claiming your entitle deductions.

Optimize your Web site for search engines to get your business seen by your audience through organic traffic. For people who wish to market online to a large network of individuals, SEO work is key. Even though you can hire a professional, there are many resources and guidelines that can enable you to do your own SEO.

Promote your home business every time you can. If you are talking to someone and the opportunity arises, don't hesitate to mention your business. Keep your business cards handy and pass them out when the opportunity arises. But pick appropriate spots so you don't come off as a bore.

Network with others in your area who own home businesses. You can use this time out of your house to learn about the network, gain publicity and show others your support as you gain support.

It's also good to meet people face-to-face and not just through your computer and or talking on the phone.

With these helpful tips, it is possible to have a successful work from home business. Your success depends on the inner drive to succeed coupled with the knowledge of how to achieve your goals. By using the above advice in these chapters, you will see your income from your work from home business flourish.

"Good luck in your endeavor it is very rewarding when done right, focus on the positive. You are on your way to achieving your goal" Christine Adindu

Disclaimer

This book details the author's personal experiences with and opinions about right-brained learning. The author is not licensed as an educational consultant, teacher, psychologist, or psychiatrist.

The author and publisher are providing this book and its contents on an "as is" basis and make no representations or warranties of any kind with respect to this book or its contents. The author and publisher disclaim all such representations and warranties, including for example warranties of merchant-ability and educational or success advice for a particular purpose. In addition, the author and publisher do not represent or warrant that the information accessible via this book is accurate, complete or current.

The statements made about products and services have not been evaluated by the U.S. and or Canadian government.

Please consult with your own legal or accounting professional regarding the suggestions and recommendations made in this book.

Except as specifically stated in this book, neither the author or publisher, nor any authors, contributors, or other representatives will be liable for damages arising out of or in connection with the use of this book. This is a comprehensive limitation of liability that applies to all damages of any kind, including (without limitation) compensatory; direct, indirect or consequential damages; loss of data, income or profit; loss of or damage to property and claims of third parties.

You understand that this book is not intended as a substitute for consultation with a licensed teacher, educational, legal or accounting professional. Before you begin any change in your lifestyle in any way, you will consult a licensed professional to ensure that you are doing what's best for your situation.

Home Cash Power - Thinking About Making Money Online?
Before you Do, You Need This Guide:
Step By Step Guide to Having Online Success Working From Home
By
Amaka C Adindu

Amaka Adindu

She is an Author/Blogger, Business Coach, Social Media Marketing Engagement Consultant. She has hands on experience from several years in business operations and management. Her focus is on helping clients get on track including Social Media visibility, build custom audience, generate leads in their niche make sales. She can help you run online campaigns, sweepstakes, giveaways, lead magnets and content creation, blogs. Creating and giving value, she has enthusiasm, lives with Passion and she is driven.

Make your DREAMS a REALITY!

Thinking About Making Money Online Working From Home?

Before you do, you need This Guide: Step By Step Guide to running a Home based business Online and or offline . These helpful tips will lead you on your way. It is possible to have a successful work from home business. Success depends on the inner drive to succeed coupled with the knowledge of how to achieve your goals. By using the advice provided in this book, you will see your income from your work from home business flourish.

By Amaka Adindu